WADO RYU KA

Patrick Stephens Limited, part of Thorsons, a division of the Collins Publishing Group, has published authoritative, quality books for enthusiasts for more than 20 years. During that time the company has established a reputation as one of the world's leading publishers of books on aviation, maritime, military, model-making, motor cycling, motoring, motor racing, railway and railway modelling, and sports and pastimes subjects. Readers or authors with suggestions for books they would like to see published are invited to write to: The Editorial Director, Patrick Stephens Limited, Thorsons Publishing Group, Wellingborough, Northamptonshire NN8 2RQ.

WADO RYU KARATE

David Mitchell

Patrick Stephens Limited

© David Mitchell 1990

All rights reserved. No part of this publication may be reproduced, stored in a retrieval system or transmitted, in any form or by any means, electronic, mechanical, photocopying, recording or otherwise, without prior permission in writing from Patrick Stephens Limited.

First published in 1990

British Library Cataloguing in Publication Data
Mitchell, David, *1944-*
Wado ryu karate.
1. Karate
I. Title
796.8153

ISBN 1-85260-280-5

Patrick Stephens Limited is part of the Thorsons Publishing Group, Wellingborough, Northamptonshire NN8 2RQ, England.

Printed in Great Britain by The Bath Press, Bath, Avon
Typesetting by MJL Limited, Hitchin, Hertfordshire.

1 3 5 7 9 10 8 6 4 2

Contents

Wado Ryu Karate	11
The Wado Ryu Club	14
The White Belt Syllabus	19
The Yellow Belt Syllabus	53
The Orange Belt Syllabus	70
The Green Belt Syllabus	92
The Purple Belt Syllabus	103
The First Brown Belt Grade	108
Brown Belt Second and First Kyu	123
Glossary	125

Dedication

I would like to dedicate this book to Leonard Sydney Palmer. In 1964, Len was one of a small group of people who laid the foundations for karate development, and it is primarily through his hard work that Wado Ryu karate has become established in Britain.

Acknowledgements

It is a great pleasure for me to acknowledge the assistance provided by Peter Spanton and John Howard of the Higashi Karate Kai in the production of this book. Peter was one of the first British Wado Ryu black belts, and it is therefore fitting that he should model for the photographs and advise me on the finer points of technique.

Wado Ryu Karate

The meaning of Wado Ryu karate

Wa exists when there is neither fear nor anger. It is the calmness that comes when the mind is not struggling with emotions. This is very much in keeping with the principles of traditional Japanese martial arts which taught that mastery over training comes only through mastery over self. **Do** is a frequently used word in many martial art traditions. It means more than just practice; it actually denotes a way of life. What it suggests is that you must follow this way in all aspects of your life — not just on training nights.

Ryu is yet another word encountered frequently in the long history of Japanese martial arts, and refers to the core of knowledge which has built up within a particular tradition over the passage of time. New masters bring their own personal interpretations to enrich the founder's original inspiration, so as time passes the tradition grows in knowledge.

Kara was a term used to describe Tang dynasty China but a desire to promote karate as wholly Japanese led to a different kanji character being selected.

Figure 1 *The actual techniques of Wado Ryu are, to some extent at least, incidental to the purpose of practice.*

Although still pronounced 'kara', it now means 'empty'. **Te** simply means 'hand', so 'empty hand' could be taken to mean that karate uses no weapons. Yet we know that this is not strictly the case, for although no weapons are taught as part of the Wado

Ryu syllabus, earlier forms of karate did use a whole arsenal of them. In fact the unarmed portion of karate was originally the less important part of training.

Another possible meaning of 'empty hand' harks back to Buddhist principles in that it suggests an absence of preconception or influence; a way of acting without malice or hysteria.

The founding of Wado Ryu karate

The founder of Wado Ryu karate was the classical Japanese martial artist Hironori Ohtsuka (1893-1982). Ohtsuka was already skilled in **Shindo Yoshin Ryu Jiu Jitsu** when he met the Okinawan karate master Gichin Funakoshi. He was impressed with karate and eventually became Funakoshi's senior student, studying a blend of styles which eventually came to be known as **Shotokan**.

Funakoshi regarded karate as a true martial art, and felt it could not be practised in a competitive way and still retain its character. Ohtsuka disagreed and wanted to test karate techniques through safe competition, so he broke away and founded Wado Ryu karate. The first Japanese karate match was held at Ohtsuka's instigation, and in the end his way prevailed, and karate competition is now widely practised in all the major karate ryu.

The Wado Ryu Association (**Wado-Kai**) was accepted into membership of the governing Japanese Karate Federation and it is now recognized as one of the four major schools.

Wado Ryu karate in Britain

Wado Ryu karate was introduced to Britain in November 1964 following a demonstration before an invited audience of kendo practitioners in Vauxhall, south-east London. The principal demonstrator was Tatsuo Suzuki, then a 7th dan and a senior student of Mr Ohtsuka. At a meeting following the demonstration, Mr Suzuki agreed to send a Japanese instructor to Britain to open clubs. In the event, he came himself, followed by Masafumi Shiomitsu (then a 4th dan) and Toru Takamizawa (then a 3rd dan).

The founding association first named itself the **Eikoku Karatedo Renmei** (English Karate Association), but even before letterheads were printed it changed its name to The British Karate Association to bring it in line with the British Judo Association.

Figure 2 *Wado Ryu karate relies as much on accuracy, speed, distancing and timing as it does on power alone.*

Someone noticed that the initials BKA could be confused with the British Kendo Association and so the title All-Britain Karate Do Association was chosen instead. The ABKA held the European mandate to represent British karate in Europe, and the first team sent consisted entirely of Wado Ryu karate practitioners.

Following a disagreement on policy, the Japanese instructors left the ABKA and founded a new group named The United Kingdom Karatedo Federation. Both associations subsequently suffered further splits and there are currently no less than 42 schools practising Wado Ryu karate in the United Kingdom.

Characteristics of Wado Ryu karate

Wado Ryu karate is one of the 'softer' styles of karate, which means that it does not rely so heavily upon physical strength. The fastest actions of all take place when muscles are relaxed, so Wado Ryu techniques are literally 'thrown' rather than thrust at the target, and the muscles only tighten as contact is made.

Wado Ryu also makes more use of body evasion than the other styles. This causes the opponent's attack to miss, yet leaves one close at hand and able immediately to counter-attack. Perhaps the best description of Wado Ryu principles came from a Japanese instructor who used the analogy of a fast-flowing stream approaching a rock. The water does not hesitate; it merely divides around the rock and rejoins smoothly afterwards. Such is the action of Wado Ryu. The opponent's move is evaded and countered in one, seamless movement.

Ohtsuka took a very liberal view of training. When a senior French karateka asked him if one performed a technique this way or that way, he replied, 'Whichever way feels better to you — that is the correct one.' This flexibility allows an element of personal adjustment to the basic teachings and explains why some coaches teach a technique one way, and others in a different way. Neither way is wrong. This is not, of course, to say that you can please yourself. If you practise Wado Ryu karate, then you will follow a set of standard principles, and such adjustments as may be made occur only in minor areas — such as the height of the non-extended fist in lunge punch.

The Wado Ryu Club

If you have not yet begun training, the first thing to do is to join a bona fide club. The address of your nearest club can be obtained from the Martial Arts Commission, 1st Floor Broadway House, 15-16 Deptford Broadway, London SE8 4PE (enclose a stamped addressed envelope if you want a prompt reply). The telephone number is 01-691 3433. The Commission holds a current register of all the authentic clubs in Britain and will be able to help you.

Bear in mind that no law governs karate practice, so anyone can buy a black belt and set up as a coach. After a short while, some students drop out of training and open their own clubs, but while they may have learned a little they will not be qualified to teach the art. Yet they will have no problem in joining an unscrupulous karate association which is not affiliated to the governing body. Associations registered with the Commission produce skilled **karateka** (people who practise karate), and those interested in teaching can take a coaching examination which ensures that they are trained to pass on their knowledge both efficiently and safely.

Karate is not one of the most expensive activities to take up. There is an initial joining fee to the club, and thereafter a nightly mat fee. You will also be required to register annually with the association to which your club is affiliated, and this includes the cost of a Martial Arts Commission licence, which incorporates a valuable personal accident/third party insurance policy.

You will need a karate suit (**karategi**), but do not buy one before joining a club as many club coaches can supply a good one more cheaply than one bought from a sports shop. Buy a size too large because karategis shrink each time they are washed. Each suit comes with a white belt and this will be suitable for the majority of clubs. Some may require you to start with a red belt, but keep the white belt anyway, because you will need it after your first grading.

At some stage you will need to buy a set of fist protectors, known colloquially as 'mitts', and these will probably be available through your club. Choose a pair which leave the thumb unpadded, and which have no more than 1cm of padding over the knuckles. Shin pads are also useful but make sure they fit comfortably and securely around your calves. 'Flip-flop' sandals are worth buying, especially if you have to walk a distance between the changing room and the training area, and a track suit will keep you warm during lulls in training.

Wado Ryu karate training is broken down into eight units known as **kyu** grades. Each unit contains a cross-section of practice, and more and more skill is needed as one progresses through the units to black belt. Classical Wado Ryu karate used only three belt colours — white, green and brown — but that is now superseded by the following:

Novice grade	3 months	Red belt
8th Kyu	3 months	White belt
7th Kyu	3 months	Yellow belt
6th Kyu	3 months	Orange belt
5th Kyu	3 months	Green belt
4th Kyu	3 months	Purple belt
3rd Kyu	3 months	Brown belt
2nd Kyu	6 months	Brown belt
1st Kyu	6 months	Brown belt

It therefore takes approximately 33 months to progress through the grades to black belt, based upon twice weekly training, with each session lasting a minimum of 90 minutes. There will also be weekend courses to cover specialized subjects in greater detail, and you should also try to attend winter and summer residential courses because they foster a spirit of identification with other association members and provide intensive training. Don't be content with training only during lessons. Train at home and your technique will improve more rapidly. Remember that successful karate training is based upon endless repetition; the more you practise the better you will become.

The coach monitors your training and corrects mistakes by repositioning your arms and legs. Try to *feel* the corrected position, so you develop an awareness of what you are doing. This reduces the need for external correction and means you will fare better at grading examinations. Mirrors are also useful for showing what you are doing, rather than what you think you are doing. Provided progress is satisfactory and you miss few or no lessons, you will learn all the required techniques well inside the grading period. Your coach will advise you when to take the grading and this generally means that, despite any feelings of unpreparedness which you may have, your techniques are up to scratch. It only remains for you to go out on the practice area and do your best. Few sensible coaches fail students!

Figure 3 *Skill progression through Wado Ryu karate is measured by the coloured belt system. The higher the grade held, the greater the personal skill level.*

A typical night's training in Wado Ryu karate

Get changed from your working clothes into your karategi and track suit. Then go to the door of the training hall (**dojo**). Pause there and face towards the senior grade. If no senior grade is present, face the centre of the room and perform a standing bow. Bring your heels together and place the flats of your hands against the front of the thighs (**4**). Incline your head and upper body forward in a smooth action; pause at the lowest point (**5**) and then return once more to an upright position. Kick off your training slippers and go on to the training floor. Warm up by running on the spot, or by gently performing karate techniques. However, do not undertake any strenuous or explosive actions at this time. Your body will take a short time to prepare for training and it is best to warm up gradually. Slip off your tracksuit when you feel warm.

When all the students have arrived, the class senior will call them to order. Everyone stands in lines according to their grade, so check to see which line is yours and join it midway along its length. This will allow you to compare what you are doing with your more experienced neighbours. The

Figure 4 *Place the flats of your hands against the front of your thighs. Your heels are together but your feet are splayed.*

Figure 5 *Bow slowly and deliberately and always look forward.*

senior grade then directs a programme of exercises designed to loosen up every joint in the body and to narrow down your attention to the evening's training. An effective training session consists of three exercise periods which are:

- The warm-up, to prepare you for training;
- Body preparation, to improve your fitness;
- The cool-down, to return you to normal levels of activity.

When the class is thoroughly prepared, the senior student joins the lines and the coach takes his position at the head. Use this time to adjust your karategi. The senior student calls out a series of commands. These are:

- **Seiza!** Drop down on to your right knee, bring in your left knee and kneel down with your back straight and ankles fully extended. Place the palms of your hands on the top of your thighs;
- **Sensei-ni-rei!** Slide your hands forward and off the front of your knees. Incline your upper body but keep looking froward. Pause at the lowest point and then return to an upright position;
- **Otogai-ni-rei!** Repeat the kneeling bow, this time to your classmates;
- **Kiritsu!** Lift your left knee, then your right, resuming a standing position with heels together and feet splayed, palms flat on the front of your thighs;
- **Rei!** Perform a standing bow and you are now ready to begin training.

The above sequence of commands is repeated at the end of the training session.
If you arrive late and the lesson has already begun, warm-up unobtrusively and then perform the two kneeling bows. Remain in the kneeling position and wait to be summoned on to the mat.

If all this seems rather strange, remember that karate is not merely a leisure, or a sporting activity. Its roots go a long way back into Japanese culture and these rituals illustrate and underline the two-way courtesy and respect which is integral to karate practice.

Training in Wado Ryu karate falls into the following categories:

- Basic techniques (**kihon**): these are the individual kicks (**keri**), punches and strikes;

Figure 6 *Kihon is the section which includes the basic punches and strikes of karate.*

- Blocks (**uke**): blocking techniques prevent an attack from reaching its target;
- Combination techniques (**renraku waza**): these are series of basic techniques, kicks and blocks performed without breaks in between;
- **Kata:** there is no commonly used English word for this. Katas are whole series of combination techniques performed at different speeds and in different directions;
- Prearranged sparring (**sanbon/ippon kumite**): this is work with a partner. He performs a set attack and you respond to it in a prearranged manner;
- Semi-free sparring (**jiu ippon kumite**): this is advanced partner work in which the attack is delivered in a more realistic way, and greater latitude is allowed in the response to it;
- Basic sparring (**kihon kumite**): despite the title, this type of sparring is very advanced, and though each move is rehearsed it looks exactly like free sparring;
- Free sparring (**jiu kumite**): this allows the free use of non-prohibited techniques in a realistic way.

Each lesson aims to cover as many topics as possible, though additional classes are given to kata because it takes a lot of time.

The following rules apply in any karate training hall:

- Do not smoke or eat in the training hall;
- Do not chew gum;
- Do not lark about;
- Do not talk loudly, or behave in an unseemly manner;
- Keep your karategi clean and in good repair;
- Do not sprawl over the floor during breaks. Sit with legs crossed, or in a kneeling position;
- Do not lean against walls or pillars. Stand straight with your arms to your sides;
- Stop what you are doing when the coach calls for attention;
- Talk only when it is necessary to exchange relevant training information;
- Treat your training partner with respect and consideration at all times.

Do not use karate skills in the street. In the hands of an expert, karate can be very dangerous, and even a small miscalculation — such as may happen in the heat of a fight — can lead to tragedy. The true karateka avoids conflict by walking away from trouble.

The White Belt Syllabus

Introduction

The white belt, or 8th kyu syllabus is the first step on a path leading to black belt, and is perhaps the most challenging grade since everything is new. The relentless repetition of basic technique is enough to drive away all but the keenest students, and perhaps this is not altogether a bad thing since it weeds out those unsuitable to learn the more practical techniques of karate.

Repetition is the *only* way to develop skill, and the harder you work at this grade the easier the next becomes.

Preliminary training

Before entering into the syllabus proper, you must learn how to make a fist and how to punch effectively. Open your hand out fully and then fold down the fingers until they touch the bar of flesh running along the top of the palm. Then close the fist, locking the index and middle fingers by folding the thumb across. Look at the top of your fist and you will see that it is uneven — the knuckles do not lie all in one line. In recognition of this, Wado Ryu karate uses only the knuckles of the index and middle fingers. This has the additional benefit of concentrating impact force through a small area, so strikes become more powerful.

Use a light punching bag to check that you are striking with the correct part of the knuckles. Strike gently at first! You may find that you cannot fold in your fingers tight enough, so they strike the bag with the middle knuckles. This is a common fault and must be corrected early on by repeated bag work, or by press-ups on closed fists. Avoid damaging your knuckle joints by pressing up from a slightly padded surface. Bag work will also show you how to position your wrist joint, so impact does not cause it to flex or twist. You will discover that the best impacts are made when the supporting bones of the two leading knuckles are in one straight line through the wrist to the two bones in the forearm. Any deviation from this straight line will cause the wrist to bend. Most karate punches use a turning action of the forearm, so the fist twists palm-downwards as contact is made. It is not necessary to use this action when punching the bag.

The basic punching action is practised

Figure 7 *Extend your left fist and turn the knuckles upwards. Pull the right fist back to your hip.*

Figure 8 *Move your arms at equal speed, so the fists pass each other at the midway point.*

from a horse-riding stance known as **kibadachi**. Step to the side with your left and right feet until they are about half as wide again as your shoulders. The feet point forwards or slightly inwards, and the knees are bent almost to a right angle. Keep your back straight, neither leaning forwards nor poking out your backside. Carry both fists on your hips, with the palms rotated upwards. This is a very tiring stance and the thighs soon begin to ache with muscular strain. By all means lift the stance slightly, or even lower it, but do not come out of it until the end of practice. It so happens that horse-riding stance is very good for strengthening the muscles which position the bones of the knee — and this is very important, bearing in mind the amount of kicking soon to be practised.

Extend your left fist and twist it so the palm turns downwards (**7**). Don't let your left shoulder lift or move forward behind the action. The extended fist is in the mid-line of the body. On the command, withdraw your left fist and simultaneously thrust out the right, so they pass each other at the midway point (**8**). As the right elbow extends the left flexes, and the first approaches the hip. In the last few instants, both fists suddenly rotate so the right fist turns palm-down and the left palm upwards (**9**). This action *must* be simultaneous. Your fists have been relaxed until now, but as imaginary impact is about to be made they clench tightly. Restrict this spasm of the muscles to the forearms.

All the punches which you will subsequently learn are based upon this combi-

THE WHITE BELT SYLLABUS

Figure 9 *The punch is fuelled by the pull back of the left arm, plus a short hip action and a shrug of the shoulders. All the muscles spasm for an instant and then relax once more*

Examine the way you are punching and see if there is any way you can make the punch stronger without leaning your shoulders into the action. Take your hip back slightly as you withdraw a fist and then twist it forward a few degrees as that same fist extends. Do not exaggerate this movement. Then do the same with your shoulders, but again, do not move more than a couple of degrees or so.

Punches

Once you can make an effective fist and know how to punch in a co-ordinated way, you are ready to begin basic training.

Lunge punch, turn and head block

Stand with your feet a shoulder-width apart and your hands closed into fists (**10**). On the command:

- Step forward a pace and a half with your left leg (**11**);
- Fully straighten your right leg, using this action to thrust the left foot forward;
- Thrust out your left fist into a punch, pulling the right back to the hip (**12**).

The stance you have just taken up is known as forward stance, or **zenkutsudachi**. It has the following characteristics:

- The right knee is fully straightened;
- The left knee is bent so that it overlies the toes;
- The right foot is twisted as far forward-facing as is comfortable;
- The left foot points directly forwards;

nation pull-back/punching action, and most beginners concentrate on the punch, ignoring the pull-back. This leads to incorrect technique which, if it is not corrected early on, is difficult to eradicate later. I recommend that you practise this action using your karate belt. Take up your stance facing an upright bar or firmly anchored pole. Pass your belt around it and grasp one end in each hand. Adjust the free length of belt held so that when one fist is extended, you have enough slack to pull the other end back to your hip. Begin slowly by putting all of your energy into pulling back the withdrawing fist. Speed up the action as you become used to it, and this will soon generate the right feel.

WADO RYU KARATE

- The left foot not only lies in front of the right, but it also lies to the left side, so the stance has an element of sidestep necessary to give stability;

- The right hip is swivelled forwards so the body is presented square on to an opponent;

- The shoulders are relaxed and the head is held high;

- The right fist is palm-upwards facing on the right hip. The left fist is turned palm-downwards;

Figure 10 *Stand in the stance known as* **yoi**, *with feet a shoulder width apart and hands closed into fists.*

Figure 11 *Extend your right fist and step forward with the left leg.*

Figure 12 *Pull back your right fist and punch with the left.*

THE WHITE BELT SYLLABUS

Figure 13 *Bring the punching fist into the centre line of your body.*

Figures 14 *Step forward in such a way as to maintain side step.*

- The left fist is brought into the centre-line of the body (**13**).

Use a mirror to check all these points if you are training at home. Take special note of the side-step you are using, which should not be so narrow as to make the stance unstable, nor so wide as to open your groin to the opponent's attack. Check by dropping your right knee to the floor and measuring the width between your right knee and your left heel. This should be equivalent to two fist-widths.

Step forward with the right foot, so that:

- Side-step is maintained (**14**);
- The right foot advances a pace and a half, accelerating all the way;
- The left leg remains bent as you step, so you do not give the appearance of bobbing up and down;
- Your shoulders remain relaxed and do not hunch;
- Your left arm remains extended and does not wave around;
- The left arm is pulled back *only* when weight descends on the right foot — neither before nor after;
- At the conclusion of the step forward, the right fist is fully extended and the left lies on the hip. (**15**).

Perhaps the two most difficult things are keeping a degree of side-step in the stance and punching at the right time to make use of the energy generated by your advancing body. Typically novices punch too early and throw themselves off balance, or they wait too long and punch once they have stopped moving, so momentum is lost.

Repeat lunge punch (**junzuki**) until you run out of space. Then practise a combination turn and head block (**mawatte**

Figure 15 *Lunge forward and punch as body movement comes to a stop.*

Figure 16 *Look over your shoulder and slide your back leg across. Notice that the heel is raised.*

Figures 17 and 18 *The blocking forearm moves diagonally upward, sweeping the face clear. The right arm is withdrawn.*

THE WHITE BELT SYLLABUS

jodan uke) in the following sequence from left lunge punch position:

- Look over your shoulder to ensure that the coast is clear and you know what you are turning into;
- Slide your right foot straight across and behind the leading leg — but do not draw it up (**16**);
- Keep your shoulders facing forwards, but begin to turn the hips so a twisting tension is set up in the spine;
- Allow the shoulders to follow the hips into the turn;
- Flex the left arm (**17**), bringing the forearm diagonally across the face so the thumb is uppermost (**18**);

- Bring the right arm forwards, forming a temporary x-block in front of the face;
- Continue the motion of the blocking forearm, so it sweeps across the front of the face and forehead. Use the left arm to supply the power for the block;
- Time the movement so the blocking forearm takes up its final position as the turn comes to a complete stop (**19** and **20**).

Head block uses a rolling action to deflect the opponent's face punch. The blocking forearm travels diagonally upwards across and away from the face. The palm is turned

Figure 19 *The blocking forearm is above and in front of the head.*

Figure 20 *The blocking forearm is above and in front of the head.*

Figure 21 *Reverse punch takes its name from the fact that the opposite fist and leg lead.*

to the floor but as final blocking position is reached, the forearm rotates so the little finger side of the fist turns upward. The following are common head block faults to avoid:

- The blocking forearm is too low, so it covers the eyes and deflects the attack into the forehead;
- The blocking forearm travels upwards but not forwards, so there is little safe distance in which to deflect the attack;
- The blocking forearm is to the side of rather than directly above the face, and so does not sweep the face effectively.

Reverse punch, turn and lower parry

Reverse punch (**gyakuzuki**) is the technique used most in all karate. It is similar to lunge punch except that the extended fist is always the opposite of the leading leg. So if the left foot leads, the reverse punch will use the right fist, and vice versa, of course (**21**). This simple difference actually leads to quite a different hip action.

Begin from left forward stance and head block as described above (**22**), then perform the following sequence of moves on the command 'Punch without stepping forward' (**sono bade ippon toru**):

- Pull back your right hip;

THE WHITE BELT SYLLABUS

Figure 22 *Reverse punch practice generally starts from a forward stance. In this case, it follows a turn/head block.*

Figure 23 *Punch without stepping forward, so your front foot pulls back and turns inwards as the right hip engages.*

- Then thrust the right hip forwards, drawing the left leg back and slightly outwards;
- Pull back the left arm and use this action to help thrust out the right fist. (**23**)

Note the following similarities/differences in posture between reverse punch stance and zenkutsudachi:

- The right knee is fully straightened;
- The left knee is bent so that it overlies the toes;
- The right foot is twisted as far forward-facing as is comfortable;

- The left foot points inwards, so it is parallel to the right;
- The left foot not only lies in front of the right, but it also lies to the left side. There is more side-step than is used in the equivalent forward stance;
- The right hip is swivelled forward so the body is presented square on to an opponent. However, because the stance is slightly wider and the leading foot turned in, the hips are turned more into the technique than they are for lunge punch;
- The shoulders are relaxed and the head is held high;

- The right fist is extended and turned palm-downwards facing. The left fist is turned palm-upwards on the left hip;
- The right fist is brought into the centre-line of the body.

Basic reverse punch is performed during an advancing movement:

- Step forwards with your left leg. This step is not direct; rather it is like a shallow 'u'. The left foot both advances and swings inwards, so it sweeps past the right ankle (**24** and **25**). Then it turns

Figures 24 and 25 *The rear foot swings inwards, as well as forwards.*

THE WHITE BELT SYLLABUS

outwards and comes to a stop, a pace and a half in front of the right;

- The outward diagonal part of the step is important both to ensure sufficient sidestep and to 'cock' the hips (**26** and **27**);
- The right foot accelerates through the step;
- The left leg remains bent, so you do not bob up and down;
- Your shoulders are relaxed and do not hunch;
- Your right arm remains extended and

Figures 26 and 27 *The outward step cocks the hips ready for the punch.*

does not wave about and it is pulled back *only* as weight descends on the right foot;

- At the conclusion of the step forward, the left hip thrusts forward. This sets up a twisting action in the muscles of the left side which helps power the punch (**28** and **29**).

Gauging the amount of side step is difficult for the novice, with stances generally too narrow or too wide, but a mirror is useful for checking this. There is a greater tendency for the leading fist to wave about during the step because the hips are used more in this technique than in the preceding lunge punch. There is also an increased tendency to bend the rear knee, or to lift the heel. Though neither of these habits will actually rob the punch of its power (all other things being equal), they are frowned

Figures 28 and 29 *The punch is generated by the stretch set up in the lateral muscles by hip movement.*

on by some purists.

Continue advancing with reverse punch until you run out of space, then turn and lower parry (**mawatte gedan barai**). To do this from a reverse punch position:

- Look over your shoulder to ensure that the coast is clear and you know what you are turning into;
- Slide your left foot straight across and behind the leading leg but don't draw it up (**30**);
- Keep your shoulders facing forwards but begin to turn the hips, so a twisting tension is set up in the spine;
- Allow the shoulders to follow the hips into the turn;

THE WHITE BELT SYLLABUS

Figure 30 *Slide your back foot across, but do not draw it up.*

Figure 31 *The left forearm flexes across the chest.*

Figure 32 *The arm then swings down in an arc, sweeping the front of the body clear.*

- Flex the extended arm, bringing the left forearm across the chest, so the little finger touches the chest (**31**);
- Keep the right fist on the hip throughout;
- Swing the blocking forearm down and across the body. Use the turning motion to supply power to the block and rotate your hips away from the blocking action, so the extended arm is helped to 'unroll';
- Time the block so the left forearm takes up its final position as the turn comes to a complete stop (**32**).

The following are common lower parry faults to avoid:

- The blocking forearm does not sweep right across the body, so a kick can still reach the left hip;
- The blocking forearm sweeps too far across the lower body, resulting in a waste of energy;
- The blocking forearm sweeps an area too far out from the body, so a low kick can still reach the pit of the stomach.

Kicks

Front kick

Front kick (**maegeri**) is typically a thrusting kick in which the ball of the foot digs into the opponent's mid-section. Before you can use this kick, you must be able to pull your foot quickly into the correct shape. Stand normally, then raise your heel as high as possible from the floor, so the toes are flexed back and the instep is in line with the shin. Keeping this shape, raise your foot from the floor and point it at the target. Bag work is essential to achieve the correct action and foot shape, since most novices either fail to pull their toes back, or they flex the ankle joint. The first fault causes toe injuries and the second robs the kick of distance and resistance to recoil. It is not necessary or even desirable to keep the kicking foot pulled into shape, since this would slow the kick. The object is to pull the foot into shape just before impact, which takes a great deal of practice.

Once you can pull back the toes, practise front kick from a fighting stance (**hanmei gamae**). Begin from attention stance by stepping a pace forward with your left foot. Settle your weight evenly between your feet and raise the left fist until it is at the height of your shoulder, carried well forward and into the projected centre-line of your body, where it can stop an attack close to source. The right fist is carried across the front of the stomach, where it provides a second line of defence and from which position a reverse punch can be quickly deployed (**34** and **35**).

The following sequence now occurs:

- Change your guard so the right arm now leads. This necessitates bringing your right shoulder forward, so a twisting stress is set up in the spine;

Figure 33 *Front kick is a powerful thrusting technique that impacts with the ball of the foot.*

THE WHITE BELT SYLLABUS

- Allow this stress to unwind by raising the right foot and bringing the right hip forward. Do not thrust off the ball of the foot, since this produces the wrong foot shape and path. Lift the foot directly, so the sole remains parallel to the floor;

- Swing the right knee forward and up, pivoting on the bent supporting leg. The supporting foot turns through 90 degrees, ensuring that the kick realizes its full range;

- The right foot hangs vertically below the knee (**36** and **37**), but as the knee comes to point just above the desired target, the knee is straightened and the foot thrust into the target;

- Keep control of body weight by slightly leaning back (**38** and **39**), but not past the point where the back of the head is vertically above the heel of the supporting foot;

- The pivoting left foot plays a major role in thrusting the kick into the target;

- Be prepared for the shock of impact, so you are not thrown backwards;

- Withdraw your foot promptly after impact is made, otherwise your opponent can seize it and jerk you off balance;

Figures 34 and 35 *Fighting stance (***hanmei gamae***) is a suitable starting stance for kicking practice. Note how the front guard hand is carried across to the centre line of the body.*

THE WHITE BELT SYLLABUS

- Set down the spent kicking foot so as to set up an effective fighting stance.

The successful kick uses one long, smooth action, rather than a series of separate moves.

The novice's front kick suffers from numerous faults, the most common being:

- Failing to change guard before kicking, which reduces hip action and shortens the kick, and is also likely to cause an awkward landing stance that is difficult to defend;
- Opening the groin as you raise the kicking knee. Keep the kicking foot near the side of the supporting leg;
- Not raising the kicking knee high enough so the kick is low;
- Straightening your supporting leg, so you bob up and down;
- Your shoulders are tense and hunch up as you kick;
- Your elbows move away from your sides;
- Your kick is off-centre;
- Losing control over your centre of gravity so the kicking foot slams down, not necessarily in the best position.

Perform a series of advancing front kicks until you run out of space. Then perform a simple turn (**mawatte**). A turn from left fighting stance is used in the following description:

- Look over your right shoulder to ensure that the coast is clear and you know what you are turning into;
- Slide your right foot straight across and behind the leading leg but don't draw it in (**40**);
- Keep your shoulders facing forward but begin to turn the hips, so a twisting tension is set up in the spine;
- Allow the shoulders to follow the hips into the turn;
- Flex the right arm, bringing the forearm across the body, so the thumb touches the chest;

Figure 40 Slide your rear foot across, lifting the heel from the floor as you do so.

Figures 36 and 37 Bring the kicking knee forward and up, closing off the groin as you do so. Note that the sole of the foot is parallel with the floor.

Figures 38 and 39 Swivel on the supporting leg and thrust out the kicking leg. Lean back but do not let your head pass behind an imaginary vertical line rising from your rear heel.

Figure 41 Bring the guarding hands powerfully across the body as the turn completes.

Figures 42 and 43 Scissors step is made with both knees bent, otherwise you will bob up and down. Maintain an effective guard.

- Pull back the left fist to power the block;

- Time the block so the right forearm takes up its final position as the turn comes to a complete stop (**41**).

The following are common faults to avoid:

- Stepping too far across with the rear foot so the new stance is too wide;

- Not stepping far enough across so the new stance is too narrow;

- Not turning strongly enough so your guard change does not function efficiently as a block;

THE WHITE BELT SYLLABUS

- Swinging your blocking arm wide of your body.

One-step front kick

As its name implies, one-step front kick (**surikomi maegeri**) uses a fast advancing step as an accelerator to close distance with the opponent; otherwise the technique is essentially the same as front kick. The distance covered by the step will depend upon the opponent's position.

Begin from left fighting stance and follow this sequence:

- Slide your right foot quickly forwards by the required distance;
- Turn your right foot so the toes point outwards. This action sets up the hips correctly (**42** and **43**);
- Keep your guard stationary and your elbows to your sides;
- Do not straighten your right leg, or you will bob up and down;
- As weight descends on the right foot, lift the left and perform front kick (**44** and **45**). Set the foot down carefully afterwards.

Note that unlike front kick on its own, the guard is not changed. This feature is common to all one-step kicks. Novices find difficulty in getting an easy step/kick transition, but everything smoothes out with practice.

Side stamping kick to the knee

Side stamping kick to the knee (**sokuto**

Figures 44 and 45 *Use the step to add power to your front kick. This means timing everything exactly right.*

fumikomi) strikes downwards with the heel of the foot. Unlike front kick, the ankle is flexed (as when you are standing normally upon it). Raise your big toe and turn the others downwards, or if you cannot manage this at first, either lift all of your toes or turn them all downwards. A little practice will soon enable you to form the correct foot position. This kick is particularly dangerous and can cause permanent damage to the opponent, and for this reason it is not permitted in free fighting, or in competition. Please bear this warning in mind.

Begin from left fighting stance, using the following sequence of moves:

- Change guard as though you were performing front kick. This sets up the hip for a powerful kick;
- Bring your right knee forward and up (**46** and **47**), drawing it across the front of your body, so you pivot on the bent left supporting leg;

Figures 46 and 47 *Bring your knee forward and up, so it closes off your body from sudden attack.*

THE WHITE BELT SYLLABUS

- The right heel is not directly below the knee, but rather it is lifted slightly and points directly at the opponent's kneecap;

- Use a combination of gravity, hip action and the muscles of the upper leg to thrust the right foot out and down. The supporting leg turns anticlockwise and the body turns sideways on to the opponent (hence the name!) (**48** and **49**);

- The body leans away from the kick, so removing the face from harm whilst counterbalancing the weight of the extending leg. This prevents you falling towards the opponent, should the kick miss;

- The right arm extends down the length of the kicking leg and the left flexes across the chest;

Figures 48 and 49 *Thrust your heel out and down, leaning back to counterbalance the weight of the extended leg. Your right arm extends down the kicking leg and the other is pulled neatly back to your side.*

- The spent kick is pulled back to the body before it is set down (**50**).

Figure 50 *Withdraw the spent kick before setting it down.*

The combination of hip twist, lean back and thrust is difficult to operate concurrently and novices usually tack one movement to the end of another, causing a jerky, weak action. The following are also common faults:

- The foot is not formed correctly so impact is made with the ball or sole;
- The supporting leg does not twist beyond 90 degrees, so the hips are not properly used and both range and power are lost;
- The kicking knee is not raised high enough, so the foot is thrust out horizontally, rather than diagonally downwards;
- The body does not lean back sufficiently, so you fall forward after the kick is retrieved;
- The spent foot is not retrieved properly, so you land in a sideways-on position to the opponent.

Practise advancing side stamping kick to the knee until you run out of space, then turn as from a front kick.

Combination techniques

Four combination techniques must be learned for white belt. These all involve front kick and either snap punch or reverse

THE WHITE BELT SYLLABUS

Figure 51 *Do not change your guard as you raise your knee in preparation for a front kick.*

Figure 52 *Perform a front kick, holding your guard as you do so.*

punch. The object is to perform them quickly and smoothly, whilst generating obvious power. Each element of the combination must be performed to a high standard.

Front kick, snap punch

The Japanese name for this sequence is **maegeri chudan, tobikomizuki jodan**. Begin from left fighting stance and follow this sequence:

- *Do not change your guard*, despite performing a basic front kick. The reason for this will be given a little later;

- Pivot on your left foot and raise your right knee, diagonally to the front (**51**);

- Perform front kick with your right leg (**52**) and set the foot down carefully to ensure a proper following stance (**53**);

- Sharply withdraw your left fist to rest position on your left hip as you are landing (not afterwards!). Use this long and powerful action to power a punch with the right fist to the opponent's face (**54**), then withdraw it immediately after contact is made with the target;

- Withdraw the punching arm only as far as front guard hand position — do not bring it back to the hip (**55**).

If you fall into the habit of changing your

guard before kicking, then the punch will have a shorter distance over which to accelerate. Try it for yourself and see! Novices frequently lose control over the spent kick in their hurry to punch, so the foot slaps down. There is also a tendency to land first and then punch. This too must be avoided because it wastes energy.

Front kick reverse punch

As if to confuse you, this sequence *does* rely on an opening change of guard to set your hips up correctly! Its Japanese name is **Maegeri chudan, gyakuzuki chudan**. Follow this sequence from left fighting stance:

Figure 53 *Your guard is unchanged even as you set down the kicking foot.*

Figure 54 *Pull back your guard hand and use this action to thrust out snap punch.*

Figure 55 *Allow natural elasticity in the elbow joint to snap back the punch.*

THE WHITE BELT SYLLABUS

Figure 56 *This time change your guard as you kick.*

Figure 57 *Perform front kick to mid-section.*

Figure 58 *Land with the hips cocked and ready to twist forward.*

- Change your guard, so the right fist moves to forward guard position (**56**);
- Perform front kick (**57**), and withdraw the foot afterwards;
- Strongly withdraw the right fist (**58**), and reverse punch with the left (**59**) as weight comes down on the front foot. Concentrate on pulling back the right hand rather than the punch;
- Withdraw the spent punch to the left hip, while returning the right fist to forward guard position (**60**).

Figure 59 *Pull back your leading guard hand and thrust out a reverse punch.*

Figure 60 *Pull back the punch with equal speed.*

The punch and pull-back can appear cumbersome if too much shoulder action is employed. Your coach will check to see whether you have used your hips to produce a smooth, fast action.

One-step front kick, snap punch

This sequence (**surikomi maegeri chudan, tobikomizuki jodan**) is similar to the first insofar as the kick and punch are both made with the same side of the body (*cf* the previous and following techniques). If you begin from left fighting stance, then you will be stepping forward with your right leg, kicking with your left foot, and punching with your left fist all the way up the training hall. Follow this sequence:

- Step forward with the right foot and perform front kick with the left leg. Do not change your guard;
- Retrieve the kick and set it down in the correct position;
- Thrust out your left fist in a punch to your opponent's face even as you are landing. Lean slightly into the punch, but not so far that you lead with your chin;
- Withdraw the punching fist to forward guard position immediately after impact is made.

One-step front kick, reverse punch

This is the final combination required for the white belt syllabus. Its Japanese name is **surikomi maegeri chudan, gyakuzuki chudan**. Learn these terms because they

THE WHITE BELT SYLLABUS

are the only ones used at a formal grading. Follow this sequence from left fighting stance:

- Step forward with the right foot and perform front kick with the left leg. Do not change the guard;
- Retrieve the kick and set it down in the correct position to cock your hips;
- Thrust out your right fist in a punch to your opponent's mid-section even as you land;
- Withdraw the punching fist to rear guard position.

Blocks

Two mid-section blocks are required for the white belt syllabus. They are performed while advancing and turning, and are always followed with a reverse punch to your opponent's mid-section.

Mid-section outer block, reverse punch

This block/reverse punch combination rejoices in the Japanese name of **chudan soto uke, gyakuzuki chudan**. Follow this sequence from left forward stance:

- Punch without stepping forward (**sono bade ippon toru**) (**61**);
- Step directly forward with the right foot. At the same time flex your right elbow and drop the forearm diagonally down and across the lower part of your body, so the thumb touches the lower left rib cage (**62** and **63**);

- The left hip is left behind during the step. This is important because it sets up the hips to generate power for the block;
- As (not after) the step comes to a stop and weight settles on the right heel, swing the right forearm up and across the body in the manner of a windscreen wiper;
- Rotate the forearm so the thumb turns outwards, as the blocking fist is sweeping across the mid-line of your chest. This happens quickly and is linked to a sharp pull-back of the left hip (**64** and **65**);
- The blocking fist is at the same level as the right shoulder. There is a 90 degree bend in the elbow and the outer

Figure 61 Punch without stepping forward, driving the hip forward and withdrawing the left arm.

WADO RYU KARATE

THE WHITE BELT SYLLABUS

side of the forearm is in line with the side of the body;

- There is the briefest of pauses as the block is completed, then the right arm is pulled back to the hip. This provides power for left reverse punch (**66**). Additional energy is provided by the left hip swinging forward. The leading foot pulls back slightly and turns inward, so the feet are parallel.

Subsequent advancing blocks use the reverse punch position as a starting point.

Note that the block is made from a forward stance and the punch from reverse punch stance. The coach looks for a clear distinction between these two, showing that the hips have been properly used. Note also that the block is powered by three actions, only one of which is immediately apparent:

- Shoulder and upper arm muscle action;
- The left hip pulling back a few degrees, so the block is unrolled. This action also extends range, involving the shoulder without slowing the block;
- The blocking arm is relaxed throughout and it only tightens as the forearm rotates.

Novices make a number of mistakes in the execution of this technique, the most common being:

Figures 62 and 63 *Step forward and drop the forearm down across the front of the body. The thumb comes to lie against your ribs.*

Figures 64 and 65 *Pull back the left hip and block outwards with your leading arm. The blocking forearm comes to a stop in front of your right shoulder.*

Figure 66 *Pause for an instant and then draw back your blocking arm, thrusting out a reverse punch to mid-section.*

- A failure in co-ordination, so the block is made only after forward movement has come to a complete stop;
- The blocking arm does not move fully across the body so the opponent's punch can still reach;
- The blocking arm moves too far across the body, wasting effort and slowing the following reverse punch;
- The blocking forearm is not sufficiently flexed, so it fails to sweep a wide area;
- The blocking forearm is flexed too much, so there is only a short distance in which to deflect the punch before it strikes;

- The blocking forearm is not rotated at the end of its sweep, so the technique lacks force;
- The block blurs immediately into the punch;
- The hips do not swing freely behind the punch, so forward stance is retained.

Continue advancing whilst blocking/punching until you run out of space. Then simply treat the turn as though it were yet another advancing step. From right reverse punch:

Figure 67 *Step across with your back leg and fold the blocking forearm across your chest.*

Figure 68 *Use the turning action of the hips to throw out the block.*

Figure 69 *Pull back your blocking arm, using this action to help power reverse punch.*

THE WHITE BELT SYLLABUS

- Look behind, then step across with your right leg;
- Swivel your hips after your shoulders;
- Bend your right elbow and fold it across your stomach (**67**);
- Use the twisting motion to aid the blocking action which begins as you are turning and finishes as the turn completes (**68**);
- Reverse punch with your left arm (**69**).

Mid-section inner block reverse punch

This block/reverse punch combination is known as **chudan uchi uke, gyakuzuki chudan**. Begin from left forward stance, then follow this sequence:

Figures 70 and 71 *The blocking forearm travels in a wide arc, coming across the body in a powerful movement.*

- Punch without stepping forward (**sono bade ippon toru**);
- Step directly forward with the right foot. At the same time flex your right elbow and draw it back to the side of your head, so the fist comes to lie near your right ear;
- The left hip is left behind during the step. This sets up the hips to power the block;
- Swing the right forearm down and across the body (**70** and **71**) as the step comes to a stop and weight settles on the right heel;
- As the blocking fist sweeps across the

Figures 72 and 73 *The blocking forearm twists suddenly as the left hip pulls back.*

Figure 74 *Drive the hip forward and perform reverse punch to mid-section.*

mid-line of your chest, rotate the forearm so the little finger turns inwards. Link this with a sharp pull-back of the left hip (**72** and **73**);

- The blocking fist is at the same level as the left shoulder. There is a 90 degree bend in the elbow and the inner side of the forearm lines up with the left side of the body;

- A brief pause follows the block, after which the right arm is pulled back to the hip. The left hip swings forward and the leading foot pulls back and turns in as reverse punch is thrust out (**74**).

The following are the most common mistakes:

- A failure in co-ordination, so the block is made only after forward movement has come to a stop;
- The blocking arm does not move fully across the body so the opponent's punch can still reach;
- The blocking arm moves too far across, so the upper body and ribs are opened to the opponent. The following reverse punch is also slowed;
- The blocking forearm is not sufficiently flexed, so it does not sweep a wide area;
- The blocking forearm is over-flexed, so it is too close to the chest;
- The blocking fist leads the forearm, so an attacking punch is knocked downwards into your ribs;
- The blocking forearm does not rotate, so it lacks force;
- The block blurs into the punch;
- The hips do not move freely behind reverse punch, so forward stance is retained.

Continue practising until you run out of space. Then once more treat the turn as if it were a step forward. From right reverse punch:

- Look behind, then step across with your right leg (**75**);
- Swivel your hips after your shoulders;
- Lift and flex your right elbow;

Figure 75 *Look over your shoulder and step across, folding your blocking forearm across your chest.*

- Use the turning action to cock the shoulder (**76**), then block (**77**);
- Reverse punch with your left arm.

The grading

After 96 hours or so of training, the average student will be ready to grade. This entails repeating the techniques which you have learned in front of the club coach, or an external grading examiner, and you will be called up, perhaps in groups of four or more. Some examiners will require you to go right through the syllabus without a pause, but more modern coaches are

Figure 76 *Cock your right shoulder by swinging the blocking arm out wide.*

Figure 77 *Then draw the blocking forearm across the body.*

interested in seeing the level of skill reached, not the extent of your physical endurance! They will ask you to perform one section of the syllabus, and then give you a rest as another group is called up.

If the examiner is the club coach, he will know your standards and a poor performance on the night may not mean an utter failure. Even when the grading is conducted by an external examiner, the club coach will doubtless be on hand to comment on your usual standard of practice. It is a poor coach indeed who encourages you to take a grading when he believes you do not yet have the required level of skill.

You will be allowed to grade when you have learned all of the techniques. If you aren't sure of some, get help well before the date of the examination. Do not try and learn them in the hours before a grading — this time is far better used to compose yourself. Technical ability is one factor in passing a grading; enthusiasm and spirit are others. Most coaches would say 'Better an enthusiastic average karateka than a laid-back elite performer.' Remember this!

The Yellow Belt Syllabus

Introduction

After 96 hours of training and a successful grading, you are now ready to begin the 7th kyu syllabus. To do this, you must learn three new basic techniques, two combinations and four sets of prearranged sparring. Additionally there is a **kata** called **pinan nidan** to learn, which consists of 29 techniques, performed one after another, at varying speeds. Lack of space makes it impossible to describe the katas of Wado Ryu, so this must be left to another book.

Punches

Both of the punches practised for yellow belt are peculiar to Wado Ryu karate, and are not seen in any of the other major Japanese styles.

Lunge punch to head, turn and lower block

Lunge punch to head begins from left forward stance, with the left fist extended. On the command:

- Step forward a pace and a half with your right leg, keeping your left fist stationary (**78** and **79**);
- Pull back your left fist and use this action to thrust out the right fist. Time this action to occur as weight settles on your right foot;
- Pull the left fist back to your chest and turn your right hip into the punch. Lean your body forward and tuck in your chin (**80** and **81**).

Note that the stance differs from basic zenkutsudachi in that:

- There is no side-step — both heels lie in one straight line;
- The leading foot points to the front and the rear foot is turned 90 degrees outwards;
- The body leans forward in a straight, diagonal line, from heel of rear leg to the tip of the rear shoulder.

The Japanese name for this technique is **Junzuki-no tsukomi**. The following faults must be avoided:

Figures 78 and 79 Step forward, keeping both knees bent.

Figures 80 and 81 Step in as well as forward and pull back your left fist. Lean forward so your body is in one straight line with the shoulder. Punch to the opponent's face.

THE YELLOW BELT SYLLABUS

- The heels are out of line, so there is either side-step or negative side-step. Avoid this by stepping forward without either bringing the leg in or swinging it out;

- The stance is too long, so the leading knee does not overlie the toes. Correct length of stance is only a pace and a half — the same as for lunge punch;

- The stance is too short. See above;

- The leading knee does not point straight ahead but leans inwards. This generally means that the hips have turned too far and instead of facing 45 degrees forward, they are almost 90 degrees from straight ahead;

- The shoulders are square on to the front. This is caused by under-using the hip on the punching side and is generally associated with side-step;

- The body is not leaning forwards in one straight line. Usually the hips either poke upwards or drop down.

Figure 82 *Punch without stepping forward.*

Also check out the faults which occur in lunge punch, because they show up here, too. For example, do not straighten your supporting leg as you step, and do not wave your fist about. Continue to advance and punch until you run out of space, then turn and perform head block from a normal forward stance, exactly as you did for lunge punch.

Reverse punch to groin, turn and lower block

This is not simply a reverse punch aimed at a lower target. Rather the whole stance is modified, but it remains a reverse punch insofar as the opposite arm and leg always lead. This technique is known by its Japanese name of **gyakuzuki no-tsukomi**.

Begin from basic lunge punch stance, using either a lower parry, a head block, or a lunge punch. On the command **sono bade ippon toru**, punch without stepping forward (**82**). As you step forward to punch:

- Bring your back foot forwards and inwards so it grazes the front (**83** and **84**), then swing it out to the side. Note that your leading foot naturally twists outwards as this happens;

- Keep your weight over the supporting leg until the advancing foot is in position. Do not turn your hips yet (**85** and **86**);

THE YELLOW BELT SYLLABUS

- Pull back the extended arm and punch with the other as weight descends upon the new leading foot (**87** and **88**).

The stance used differs from orthodox reverse punch stance in that:

- It is very wide in relation to its length;
- The toes of the rear foot are in line with the heel of the leading foot. Both feet are turned inwards and converge slightly;
- The body leans forward behind the punch.

Figures 83 and 84 *Bring your back foot forward and in so it grazes the supporting leg. Keep your punching arm extended and do not wave it about.*

Figures 85 and 86 *Place your foot to the side and cock your hips, ready for the punch.*

Figures 87 and 88 *Thrust your hip forward as you pull back the leading fist. Lean behind the punch but lift your head up and look forward.*

Punch delivery is co-ordinated with:

- Weight descending on to the front foot;
- Hip action coupled with forward lean;
- Pull-back of the leading fist.

Common faults are:

- The leading heel is too far in front of the toes of the rear foot. In other words, you have stepped too far forwards;
- The feet are not converging. This is caused by either not using enough hip action, or allowing the leading foot to turn outwards;

- The stance is too wide. This makes the front knee drop inwards. Push the knee outwards, so it is vertically above the foot;
- The hips are not turned fully behind the punch. Gyakuzuki no-tsukomi uses more hip twist than orthodox reverse punch. There is also more shoulder involvement, though not so much as to make the balance precarious. You should not topple forwards if the coach pulls your extended arm;
- The body does not lean forward sufficiently;
- The leading arm waves about during the step;
- The head is lowered. Lift your head and look forward.

Kicks

Your hips will be more mobile after three months' training, and it is now appropriate to learn a new kick in which this suppleness is required.

Roundhouse kick to mid-section

This is a very common kick which can be delivered either with the ball of the foot (**89**), or with the toes pointing. Traditionally the latter version is learned first. As its name implies, roundhouse kick travels along a horizontal and circular path, striking the target from the side. Do not use this kick to attack facing targets; attack the ribs, or the side of the jaw instead. The Japanese name for this technique is **mawashigeri-chudan**.

Begin from left fighting stance and:

Figure 89 *Roundhouse kick with ball of foot is not often used in classical Wado Ryu.*

Figure 90 *Move your shoulder forwards and bring up the kicking leg.*

THE YELLOW BELT SYLLABUS

- Simultaneously twist your right shoulder forward, lift your right foot, point your toes, and pivot outwards on the supporting foot;

- Lift your right knee upwards, forward *and outwards* in one fluid movement. Allow your right hip to move naturally behind the shoulders (**90**);

- Lean well back and continue to turn so your right side faces the opponent. This helps to draw the kicking hip around, so that the right knee is brought across the front of the body (**91** and **92**). The supporting leg has pivoted by at least 90 degrees at this stage;

- Thrust the right foot out horizontally as the knee is about to reach maximum height (**93** and **94**);

- Tighten the lower leg muscles as the foot is about to make contact, then pull it back before the opponent can seize hold of it;

- Put the foot down in such a way as to set up an effective fighting stance.

Notice that the kicking action begins when the shoulders set up a twisting pull in the spine as they swing around, making it easy to raise the kicking hip. The more the shoulders turn, the more powerful the kick becomes. However, it is possible to turn the

Figures 91 and 92 *Pivot on your supporting leg and lean back, bringing the kicking knee across your body in a fend off position. Point your toes.*

Figures 93 and 94 *Swing your lower leg out forcefully whilst maintaining an effective guard. Kick right across the front of your body.*

shoulders only slightly, yet still perform the technique, though this leaves the body facing forward and more vulnerable to a counter-technique.

The following are common faults of roundhouse kick:

- The shoulders do not twist, so the supporting leg does not easily rotate;
- The guard does not change, so hip action is slowed;
- The supporting leg does not pivot, so hip action is impeded and the technique becomes rather like a diagonal front kick;
- The kicking knee does not lift high enough, so the kick is low. Sometimes the novice tries to compensate for this by over-rotating the hips, but this causes the kicking knee to face down to the floor which makes matters worse!
- The kicking foot does not tense on impact. Turn the toes down hard to reduce the risk of ankle injury;
- The body does not lean back, so control over the centre of gravity is lost and the kicking foot virtually falls to the floor;
- The arms fly about and an effective guard is lost.

Refer also to the faults associated with front kick and pick out those which are common to both techniques.

Combination techniques

There are two combination techniques to be learned for yellow belt.

Front kick, roundhouse kick, reverse punch

This is a smooth, free-flowing combination

THE YELLOW BELT SYLLABUS

Figure 95 *Begin with a front kick to mid-section.*

Figure 96 *Land forward, with weight over the front foot.*

Figure 97 *Lift off the rear foot and swivel your hips, performing roundhouse kick to mid-section.*

designed to train hip action. Its Japanese name is **maegeri-chudan, mawashigeri-chudan, gyakuzuki-chudan**. Begin from left fighting stance and follow this sequence:

- Change your guard and bring your right knee up and forward;
- Thrust out your right foot in a mid-section front kick (**95**);
- Withdraw the kicking foot and set it down carefully (**96**);
- Change your guard once more as your weight settles on the right foot. Lead with your left shoulder and bring your left knee diagonally up and across the front of your body. Your supporting foot now turns outwards as the hips are brought into play;
- Lean back and deliver the kick, (**97**)

Figure 98 Set your foot down so as to cock the hips ready for a powerful reverse punch.

Figure 99 Thrust out your fist and withdraw it promptly afterwards.

then set your foot down carefully; (**98**)

- Withdraw your left arm and thrust the right fist out in a reverse punch. (**99**) Pull it sharply back to the right hip and return the left fist to forward guard position once more.

The entire sequence must be performed smoothly throughout. Inadequately supple hips will cause a jerky action.

The following are common faults:

- Failing to change your guard appropriately;
- Hesitating between kicks;
- Blurring one kick into the next;
- Failing to use the hips on the closing reverse punch, so only shoulder action occurs. Aim to make the reverse punch the most powerful technique of the three.

One-step front kick, roundhouse kick, reverse punch

This is similar to the first combination, except that it opens with a one-step front kick, so there is no need initially to change guard. However, once this first technique has been performed, the guard must be changed for the following roundhouse kick. Use the one-step as an accelerator and finish with a powerful reverse punch.

The Japanese name for this technique is **surikomi-maegeri chudan, mawashigeri-chudan, gyakuzuki-chudan.**

Blocks

No new blocks are taught in this part of the syllabus.

Prearranged sparring

Prearranged sparring introduces the concepts of timing, distance, accuracy and control in a way that is safe. Since the attacker knows which technique to use and the defender understands exactly how to respond, both can practise their techniques in a realistic manner. It is, however, a good idea to decide which partner is going to do what. Generally you should perform two or three repetitions each before changing role.

Begin with a standing bow towards each other, then move into your stances. Custom is that the defender steps back into stance while the attacker steps forward, but this is not always observed. The attacker inches gradually into range, and settles down before launching his attack. The defender must detect the attack at the earliest time to be able to respond effectively to it, and there are two ways to do this. The first suggests that you look into the opponent's eyes and try to see the reflex narrowing that takes place before any committed action is made. The second advocates an unfocused gaze that takes in the whole of the opponent's body. See which works best for you.

One-step sparring (**ippon kumite**) involves only one attack, followed by an immediate block and counter. Three-step sparring (**sanbon kumite**) uses three identical attacks, one after the other, and is especially good for teaching timing and distancing. If you block three times in every sequence, it stands to reason that you get proportionately more skill practice.

The four examples chosen are three-step sequences, in which the first two moves are blocks alone and the third is a block followed by a counter.

Mid-section outer block sequence

The opponent begins from right fighting, or forward stance, and steps forward to deliver lunge punch to the centre of your chest. The punch must be on target, otherwise you will learn how to block an off-centre punch! The speed of attack must be related to your skill level. The attacker performs one punch and allows time for your response to be made before going on with the second.

The attacker's sequence is therefore:

- Punch with left fist;
- Punch with right fist;
- Punch with left fist.

Respond by taking the corresponding step back and using outer block to deflect the attack. Since you also begin from left stance, the sequence is:

- Block with right arm (**100**);
- Block with left arm (**101**);
- Block with right arm (**102**).

Figure 100 Block outwards with your right forearm from a forward stance.

Figure 101 Take a full step back and block with the left arm.

Figure 102 Take a further step back and block with the right arm once more.

Figure 103 Circle your wrist and seize the opponent's outstretched arm. Step up with your back leg to set distance.

THE YELLOW BELT SYLLABUS

Figure 104 *Front kick with your leading leg to the opponent's ribs.*

Figure 105 *Release his arm and drop forward into a reverse punch.*

The counter-attack begins with the right fist opening and the forearm rotating so the opponent's wrist is grasped and pulled forward. Keep hold of the opponent as you slide up the back leg (**103**), and front kick with your right leg to the opponent's ribs (**104**). The purpose of the sliding step is to adjust range for the following kick. Continue to pull on the opponent's outstretched arm and perform a left reverse punch to his exposed ribs. Release your grasp when the punch strikes home (**105**) and withdraw a full step into left fighting stance. The opponent also steps back and both parties end up by facing each other once more. Keep your fists clenched, lower the guards and slowly withdraw your leading legs until you are both facing towards each other in ready stance. There is no need to bow again at this time. When you have the hang of this sequence, change sides so you both begin from left stance.

Mid-section inner block sequence

This begins in the same way as the previous sequence. Once again there are three attacks with three responses made to them, but this time inner block is used.

From the third blocking position (**106**), you:

- Spring forward with the left leg, using a thrusting action of the rear foot. Your body turns sideways on into right straddle stance:

- As your body is moving forwards, bring your left forearm across the chest with the palm facing downwards. The right forearm is parallel facing downwards, but lower down on the torso.

Figure 106 *Block his forearm and turn your hips slightly.*

Figure 107 *Turn fully sideways and drive your left elbow into the opponent's ribs.*

- As weight settles, pull your right arm back to your hip, using this action to help thrust the left elbow into the opponent's ribs (**107**).

Figure 108 *Step outwards with your front foot to take your body out of the line of the kick.*

Figure 109 *Twist your hips, using this action to bat his leg to the side.*

This sequence suffers from a common fault in that the blocking action tends to rotate the stance from forward facing to straddle. Novices also have difficulty in timing the

THE YELLOW BELT SYLLABUS

Figure 110 *Turn your hips back, behind a punch to mid-section.*

elbow strike to correspond with the spring forward.

Front kick-outer parry

This proceeds exactly as for the preceding pair, except that here the attack used is a front kick. Begin from left stance, with the opponent launching three successive kicks. Retreat before the first two, changing guard appropriately as you do so.

On the third kick:

- Do not step backwards, but instead step outwards with the leading left leg (**108**) and twist your hips. This turns your body almost parallel to the attack;
- Bring your left forearm down and smack the side of the opponent's shin, so his kick is deflected away from you (**109**);
- Give him no time to recover and per-form a right reverse punch to his kidneys (**110**), or to the back of his head;
- Take a full step back. The opponent steps diagonally through with his right leg and twists around to face you.

This block (**soto harai uke**) uses the body's twisting action to assist the deflection.
The following faults are common:

- You step too far to the side and become too far away to counter-attack swiftly. Step only by the smallest amount consistent with making the kick miss;
- You fail to step far enough to the side, so the kick catches you in the ribs. If you do not side-step at all, then his foot may strike you in the stomach. Regard the side-step as the first line of defence and the block simply as insurance;
- You do not twist your hips sufficiently, and take up straddle stance. This hinders the powerful hip action needed both by the block and the reverse punch;
- You fail to use your hips in the reverse punch, so weakening it;
- You leave it too late to launch the counter-attack.

Front kick inner parry

This uses opposite fighting stances so that if the opponent begins from left, you take up right fighting stance. The previous block is now unsafe because that same side-step puts you into a vulnerable position in which you can easily be attacked.

Begin as before, retreating before the first two kicks but on the third:

- Step diagonally back and out with your trailing left leg, drawing the right foot to it (**111**);

- Twist so your back turns three-quarters on to the opponent. At the same time block down and around with your right arm, striking the side of his shin. Pull your left arm to your chest (**112**);

- Thrust your right foot back out and turn your hips, using this action to help power a left reverse punch to the opponent's kidneys (**113**) or the back of the head.

This block (**uchi harai uke**) is quite similar to a lower parry and relies on body rotation to generate most of the power. The following are common faults:

- Failing to twist away sufficiently. This weakens the block;

- Failing to draw up the right leg. The opponent may land on your outstretched leg!

- Failing to re-extend the right leg by the

Figure 111 *Step diagonally back with your rear foot and draw the other to it.*

Figure 112 *Parry downwards with your right arm as you turn your hips and lean away from the kick. Note that the knees are brought close together.*

Figure 113 *Slide your foot back and turn your hips into a reverse punch to mid-section.*

correct amount, so you are either too close to or too far from the opponent;
- Failing to twist the hips behind the reverse punch.

Free sparring

Traditionally in western schools, this is the point at which free sparring (**jiu kumite**) is introduced, but I strongly advise against this. In my opinion, free sparring should not be practised until you have developed control and can form your techniques properly.

Most injuries in karate occur during free sparring and it is therefore ludicrous to attempt it until you have sufficient skill. Rather than set a grade limit, I would recommend that each case is taken on its merits. Some will be ready to free spar by 6th kyu, others not until 3rd kyu. I will therefore defer it until later in the book.

The Orange Belt Syllabus

Introduction

Orange belt syllabus introduces a new punch, a variation of a kick we practised earlier, some new combinations and the first of a sequence of prearranged sparring using head blocks followed by a counter. Free sparring may be introduced at this grade, providing you can perform basic techniques skilfully with control. You are required to learn the katas **pinan shodan** and **pinan sandan**.

Punches

Front kick, lunge punch

This is actually a combination technique built up of two basic moves. Its Japanese name is **kette junzuki**. The sequence is performed in the following manner:

- Begin from left lunge punch stance (**114**) by performing a front kick to mid section. Keep the punching arm still and aimed to the correct height, so the kick thrusts out just below it (**115**);

THE ORANGE BELT SYLLABUS

- Withdraw the kick sharply and set the foot down carefully;
- Pull your left fist back as weight descends on the right heel, using this action to help thrust out a right lunge punch (**116**).

Figure 114 *Begin from lunge punch stance.*

Figure 115 *Front kick, so the foot passes just underneath the extended fist.*

Figure 116 *Keep your fist extended until you land in a forward position. Then lunge punch.*

Watch out for the following mistakes:

- Kicking too low, which leaves a large gap between your extended fist and the kicking foot;
- Waving the punching arm about during the kick. The body tends to lean back during the kick and this causes the punching arm to rise;
- Allowing your shoulders to hunch up as you kick. Keep them relaxed;
- Allowing the non-punching arm to

Figures 117, 118 and 119 *Begin from reverse punch position, then front kick. Reverse punch on landing.*

swing away from the ribs. Keep it to your side;

- Mistiming the punch as weight descends on the front foot and either throwing yourself forward, or punching late and robbing the punch of power. Time it right and you will add your body's momentum to the impact power.

Front kick, reverse punch

This is very similar to the preceding technique except that you begin from reverse

THE ORANGE BELT SYLLABUS

punch position (**117, 118** and **119**).

Snap punch

We came across this technique in the very first 8th kyu combination but here we practise it on its own. Begin from ready stance by sliding your left foot forward by half a pace. There is no side-step and your fists remain by your sides. Keep your weight

Figure 120 *Take up* **shizentai** *stance, with one foot leading slightly.*

over the rear foot and relax your shoulders. The leading foot faces directly to the front and the rear foot is rotated slightly outwards. The Japanese name for this stance is **hidari** (or **migi** if the right foot leads (**120**)) **shizentai**.

On the command:

- Thrust with the left foot and allow the leading leg to slide forward by about a pace and a half (**121**);

- The back leg extends fully, so the knee straightens. The front knee bends, so it overlies the toes;

- Raise both arms forward and up, so the right fist leads and both elbows are bent with the palms turned upwards;

- Throw both fists forward as the slide comes to a stop. Pull the left back sharply and lead with the right shoulder, using these two actions to help propel the punch (**122**);

- The natural elasticity of your upper arm muscles will jerk back the spent punch. Hesitate for a second or so and then draw up the rear foot into a new shizentai position;

- Lower both arms slowly back to your sides and prepare to perform snap punches, as directed.

The sliding advance provides most of snap punch's impact energy. Less is provided by straightening the punching elbow, but if you co-ordinate the move correctly your punching arm is already straight as the advance comes to a stop. Do not stop moving and then try to punch. Hold your position for a second or so once the punch has snapped back, then drop both arms and slide the rear leg forward in a smooth, unhurried manner.

Check out the following faults:

- Lack of forward thrust. Correct this by

Figure 121 *Slide your front foot forward by a full pace and raise your fists.*

THE ORANGE BELT SYLLABUS

Figure 122 *Lean into the punch, pulling back the non-punching arm and driving the punching shoulder forward. Do not lead with your chin!*

pushing forward with the partially flexed rear knee while resisting with the leading foot. Just lift the leading foot slightly and you will surge forward;

- Telegraphing the push forward because you have obviously to change your centre of gravity before you can begin the punch proper. Some people initially lift the leading foot too high;

- The chin leads when your punching shoulder is not brought forward. Your upper body must be turned three-quarters on;

- Most novices withdraw too quickly from the completed punch position.

Repeated snap punches cover ground and when you run out of space, look over your right shoulder and slide your right foot across and behind the leading foot. Twist your hips, then after a momentary lag allow the shoulders to turn behind them. You are now facing in the reverse direction, with the other foot leading. Repeat the techniques on the right side.

The Japanese name for this technique is **tobikomizuki**.

Kicks
Side kick to mid-section

This is the only new kick to learn for orange belt, and it is similar to side stamping kick to the knee, a technique which we practised in the white belt syllabus. The Japanese name for this technique is **sokuto-chudan**. We also develop roundhouse kick by using it with a step forward.

Begin from left fighting stance and follow this sequence:

- Change your guard and bring your right

Figures 123 and 124 *Raise your rear leg, bringing the knee forward and up. Change guard and pivot on your supporting leg.*

Figure 125 *Raise your knee to the correct height, so your heel is pointing directly at the target.*

shoulder forward. Twist your supporting leg outwards slightly and raise your kicking foot;

- Bring your right knee up and forwards, whilst pivoting all the while on your supporting foot (**123** and **124**);
- Bring your right knee diagonally across your chest and point your heel towards the target (**125**);
- Thrust your foot out in a straight line to the target and lean back to control your centre of gravity (**126** and **127**).

THE ORANGE BELT SYLLABUS

Allow your supporting foot to rotate up to 180 degrees;

- Arch your back and look along the full length of your body and leg. Carry your right arm along the top of the extended leg and flex the left across your chest;
- Draw your right knee back to your chest and put the foot down so as to set up an effective fighting stance.

Power for the kicking action comes from the thrusting out of the foot combined with rotation of the hips, and to achieve maximum benefit, these must flow into each other without hesitation or jerkiness. For added penetration, drag the supporting foot forward, using momentum generated by the extending leg. This also gives a slight bonus in range and soaks up the recoil of impact. Practise this kick against a heavier punch bag, or against one that is steadied by a partner. This will show up the effects of recoil and help you to get the correct foot position.

The following are common faults:

- Hesitating between bringing up the rear knee and thrusting out the kick;
- Not twisting sufficiently on the supporting foot, so range and penetration are lost. Maximum thrust is developed when the back is turned towards the opponent;
- Not arching the back correctly, so penetration is lost;
- Not raising the kicking knee high enough, so the foot swings upwards instead of thrusting out horizontally;
- Failing to lean back, so the used kick thumps down willy-nilly;
- Not forming the kicking foot correctly, so the sole of the foot strikes the target. Lead with the heel.

Figures 126 and 127 *Thrust your heel out in a straight line, leaning well back to counter the weight of your extended leg. Maintain an effective guard throughout.*

One-step roundhouse kick

One-step roundhouse kick (**surikomi mawashigeri chudan**) is similar to the basic technique previously practised except that a one-step accelerator is used to close range. Follow this sequence from left fighting stance:

- Step forward in a scissors movement with the right leg (**128**), adjusting the length of the step to suit the distance to be closed;
- Time the kicking action so there is no hesitation between the end of the step forward and the beginning of the kick (**129** and **130**);
- Withdraw the spent kick and set it down carefully.

Remember, as with any one-step kick there is no need to change the guard. An orthodox scissors step is used where the advancing foot passes across the shin of the supporting leg.

Figure 128 *Scissors step forward, the rear leg advancing past the front of the supporting leg.*

Combination techniques

Orange belt requirement is for two combinations, both of which exploit the newly learned side thrust kick to mid-section.

Front kick, side thrust kick and reverse punch to mid-section

The Japanese name for this technique is **maegeri chudan, sokuto chudan, gyakuzuki chudan**.
Follow this sequence from fighting stance:

- Perform a front kick to mid-section, changing your guard as you do so (**131**). Land poised in a forward position;
- Raise the right foot diagonally forward and up, so it crosses the front of the lower body with the heel leading;
- Thrust out side kick to mid-section (**132**), then withdraw it and set the foot down in a forward position;
- Use the energy of a controlled landing to thrust out a reserve punch to mid-section (**133**). Withdraw the punch smartly, returning to fighting stance once more.

THE ORANGE BELT SYLLABUS

Figure 129 *Raise your kicking knee, bringing it across the front of your chest.*

Figure 130 *Thrust the kick out in one smooth movement.*

Figure 131 *Perform front kick, then land poised in a forward position.*

Figure 132 *Thrust out side kick to mid-section, then withdraw and set it down with the hips cocked to perform a reverse punch.*

Figure 133 *Make the final reverse punch the most powerful part of the sequence.*

The correct sequence builds in power and speed with each technique, but many novices run out of steam with the result that the final reverse punch is weak and ineffective. The following are also common mistakes:

- Failing to withdraw the spent front kick, so control over centre of gravity is lost and the foot slaps down;

- Hesitating between front kick and side kick, which wastes energy and produces a jerky sequence. One technique should move smoothly into the next;

- Natural spring in the elbow joint is replaced by the shoulders dragging the spent punch back after impact has been made.

One-step front kick, side kick reverse punch

The Japanese name for this combination is **surikomi maegeri chudan, sokuto chudan, gyakuzuki chudan**. It is performed in a similar manner to the above, except that a one-step accelerator is used to prime the front kick. There will be a greater tendency for the elbows to fly out from the ribs during the step.

Blocks

No new blocks are formally taught in this part of the syllabus but one of the two katas which you must perform — **pinan shodan** — contains a knife block performed from back stance and an augmented forearm block from forward stance. Since we do not cover the katas in this book, it is appropriate to lift out the two blocks and examine them at this point.

Knife block from back stance

Knife block (**shuto-uke**) uses the edge of the hand on the little finger side in a wiping action that sweeps the upper chest and face clear. Back stance (**kokutsudachi**) is particularly suitable for this block because it sets up the shoulders for a powerful action. Let's begin by looking at the characteristics of this stance:

- Weight is biased towards the rear, and only 30 per cent rests on the front foot. This is achieved by drawing the body back over the rear foot;

- The heels are in line and the front foot points forward, with heel raised from the floor. The rear foot is turned at least 90 degrees from the front;

- The rear knee is bent more than the front knee yet the body remains per-

THE ORANGE BELT SYLLABUS

fectly upright. The hips are almost 90 degrees away from forward-facing.

The following are typical faults:

- Weight bias is incorrect and generally 50 per cent rests on the front foot. Shift body weight back towards the rear foot;
- The front foot lies flat on the floor. Although this is correct in some styles of karate, it is a fault in Wado Ryu;
- The heels are not in line. Check by using a floorboard, taped line or mirror;
- The hips are not turned correctly, so either the body is too square on to the front, or it is turned too far away and the leading knee is pulled inwards.

Set the stance up and feel what it is like to hold the correct position. This will help you to self-correct as you practise stepping from one stance into another. Once you can do this freely, you are ready to combine it with the blocking action.

Begin from left back stance. Bend your left elbow through 90 degrees, raising the upper arm, so it is horizontal. You will also need to bring your elbow inwards slightly,

Figures 134 and 135 *Begin from back stance, with 75 per cent of body weight carried by the rear leg. The knife block is vertical and the other hand is held open, with the fingers pointing and the palm facing upwards.*

otherwise it will poke out to the side. Turn your forearm so the palm faces forward, and extend your fingers. Flex your thumb across the palm. Bend your right elbow and extend your hand, turning it palm upwards so the fingertips point at the left elbow. (**134** and **135**).

The following are typical faults of knife block:

- The fingers of the blocking hand do not point upwards, but rather lean to one side or another. A *slight* forward lean is permissible as long as it is not pronounced;

Figures 136 and 137 *Step forward and drop the blocking arm, bringing the other to the side of your head.*

- The blocking elbow sticks out to the side. Bring it in line with the side of your chest;
- The right wrist is bent, so the fingers point upwards. Fully extend the wrist joint.

Step into right back stance and as you do:

- Drop your left arm forward, so the palm faces the floor (**136** and **137**);
- Bring your right palm across to your left ear;
- Draw your left arm back to chest whilst cutting outwards and across with the right. Rotate both forearms together, so the right palm turns forward and the left turns upwards. (**138** and **139**).

THE ORANGE BELT SYLLABUS

The blocking action is smooth, fast and relaxed. Ensure that the block really does sweep across your face and upper body, otherwise it may allow an attack to pass through. The only tension occurs as the forearms rotate and this is followed by immediate relaxation.

The following are common faults:

- Failure to turn the shoulders in the opposite direction to the blocking action, which makes the block less able to resist recoil;
- The blocking hand does not point straight upwards;

Augmented forearm, block

The word augmented simply means made stronger, and in this method the non-blocking arm is used to add extra power to outer forearm block. Augmented block **(morote-uke)** can be practised from either back stance or forward stance; for our purposes we will use the latter.

Begin from left forward stance and raise your left arm into the completed position for mid-section outer block. The right arm rests on your hip. Step forward into right stance and as you do:

- Drop your left fist down to your left hip. Lower your right arm diagonally down and across your stomach, so the right fist lies near the left fist (**140**);

Figures 138 and 139 *Draw back the other hand and knife block.*

Figure 140 *Withdraw the blocking hip and drop both arms to your side.*

Figure 141 *Swing both arms up, turning the upper body behind the action.*

Figure 142 *Step back and make early contact with the opponent's advancing punch.*

- As weight settles on the leading leg swing both arms up in an arc across the chest;
- Tense both fists as contact is made, locking the right in a normal outer mid-section block position and bring the left across so it points at the right elbow. Keep the left elbow close to your side (**141**).

Note that whereas normal forearm block

uses an unrolling action of the shoulders, augmented block throws the shoulders into the block.

The following are common faults:

- Waiting until forward movement has ceased before beginning the blocking action. Use momentum to make the block more powerful;
- Hunching the shoulders as the arms move across the body. The shoulders stay low to concentrate power;
- Letting the blocking elbow move away from the side of the chest. This weakens the block and prevents it from sweeping the body clear.

Prearranged sparring

Four prearranged sparring sequences figure in the 6th kyu syllabus. Two are in response to a punch to the head, and two are in response to a front kick, and they may be performed as either three-step or one-step routines.

Head block I

This sequence is known as **jodan uke ipponme** and it involves a quite complicated twisting, deflection block combined with a simultaneous strike. Both partners take up left fighting stance. The attacker steps forward, accelerating into a classic lunge punch to the height of your forehead. Range should be such that if you fail to move, the punch will strike the target. This may sound a little hazardous but it is essential if you want to learn a valid block response. If this is a three-step routine, then repeat the lunge punch/head block defence. If it is a one-step sequence, then counter-attack on the first move.

Step back into right stance as the attacker advances to punch, so the correct distance between you is maintained and your opponent does not close on you. Then follow this sequence:

- Open out your left hand as you step back and your knuckles make contact with your opponent's punching arm (**142**);
- Step directly behind your right foot, lifting your heel clear of the floor. The distance which you step will affect your final position in the counter-attack response;
- Once your left foot is positioned correctly, then twist your hips into horse riding stance. This action also turns

Figure 143 *Swivel your hips into a straddle stance, taking his punch across the front of your body whilst punching him on the chin.*

your shoulders so the back of your left wrist deflects the opponents's punch past the front of your chest, as your right fist swings up in an uppercut to his jaw (**143**);

- Turn the fingers of your blocking hand outward, pressing the back of the hand against the opponent's wrist;

- Twist your hips back around and step diagonally forwards on your right foot, so you take up forward stance. Thrust your left elbow into the opponent's ribs in a horizontal circular strike (**144**);

- Pause for a second in this position, then withdraw into fighting stances.

Avoid the following mistakes:

- Beginning from an incorrect distance puts out everything that follows. Novices make an incorrect step back, so they are either too far away to block effectively, or are too close and step on each other's feet;

- The horse riding stance must be stable (pardon the pun!) if your deflection is to work. Many novices lean back, so deflection is weakened;

- Do not throw your arms too wide as you block/punch;

- If you find that your are too far away to deliver the elbow strike, then draw up your rear foot, so stance length does not elongate. Do not lean forward with your chin!

Head block II

The Japanese name for this technique is **jodan uke nihonme**. It involves a high-level block that also functions as the counterattack, so counter and response occur immediately.

Begin from opposite stance, so the attacker steps forward into left stance and you step back into right fighting stance. Then follow this sequence:

- The attacker steps forward to perform right lunge punch to your face. Maintain your guard and step straight back, so your feet come alongside each other (**145**);

- As your opponent throws his punch, step diagonally back and outwards with your right foot, so you move 45 degrees out of alignment with the attack;

- Drop into a horse riding stance and punch into the opponent's jaw. This catches his punch, deflecting it up and over your blocking forearm before carrying on into the side of his jaw (**146**);

- Twist your hips so they turn to face the

Figure 144 *Step to the side and turn your hips into a horizontal elbow strike.*

THE ORANGE BELT SYLLABUS

Figure 145 *Step straight back, so your feet come close to each other.*

opponent and seize his shoulders with your outstretched hands (**147**). Pull him forward and down and perform a rising knee kick with your right leg (**148**);

Figure 146 *Then step to the side and drop into a straddle stance. Punch up and around with your left fist, knocking his punch to one side and carrying on into his jaw.*

Figure 147 *Turn your hips forward and seize his shoulders with both hands.*

Figure 148 *Draw the opponent's upper body forward and deliver a knee strike to his polar plexus.*

- Pause, then move deliberately apart and resume fighting stances.

Watch out for the following errors:

- Stepping diagonally back at the outset, instead of first bringing the feet together. This cues the opponent, so he can re-aim his punch to your new position;
- Not judging the distance correctly so the punch can reach. The purpose of the diagonal step is to take you out of the direct line, whilst leaving you close enough to counter-attack;
- Not holding the elbow high — almost as though you were performing a head block — so the punch can be deflected over the blocking forearm. The punch is made with the little finger side of the fist pointing upwards.

Kicking block III

The Japanese name for his technique is **maegeri, soto harai uke sanbonme**. It uses the same block as maegeri soto harai uke ipponme except that the attack takes the form of a one-step kick.

Begin from left fighting stances, adjusting your distance apart so a front kick would just be out of range. Then follow this sequence:

- Withdraw your leading foot as the opponent takes a step forward. Bring both feet together;
- Step diagonally back with your right foot as the opponent performs front kick. This takes you out of the direct line (**149**);
- Strongly twist your hips and block his foot by curling your left hand under it.

Figure 149 *Step diagonally back with your front foot, maintaining an effective guard as you do so.*

Figure 150 *Turn your hips behind a deflection block that curls under and lifts his outstretched leg.*

Lift his foot slightly and knock it away from you (**150**);

- Swivel on both feet so your body turns almost completely around and you are facing parallel to the kick;

- Twist back to your original position and use this action to help thrust out a reverse punch into the attacker's back;

- Pause, then withdraw to a safe distance and take up fighting stance.

The reverse punch must follow on immediately after the block, and before the opponent can set his kicking foot down. A considerable benefit derives from using the energy of his drop forward to add impact to your punch.

Most of the faults of the first kicking block apply to this one too, so re-read the relevant parts of the previous chapter, and in addition note the following:

- Blocking with extended fingers can cause dislocations and fractures, so always block with a closed fist;

- Block under and in the direction that the kick is travelling. Do not meet the kick full on with your wrist!

- Do not knock the opponent's foot too far to the side or you will not be able to reach him with the following punch;

- Do not lean forwards as you block and punch.

Kicking block IV

The Japanese name for this technique is **maegeri uchi harai uke yonhonme**. It is identical to maegeri uchi harai uke nihonme except that a one-step front kick is used as the attack. Begin from opposite stances and follow this sequence:

- Withdraw your leading foot as the

Figure 151 *Withdraw your leading foot as the opponent steps forward.*

Figure 152 *Turn your hips away from the opponent as he kicks, and deflect his kick with* **uchi harai uke**.

opponent steps forward. Bring both feet together (**151**);

- Step diagonally back with your right foot as the opponent performs front kick. This takes you out of the direct line;
- Strongly twist your hips and block his foot with your left hand;
- Swivel on both feet so you virtually turn your back on the opponent (**152**);
- Slide your left foot back and twist your hips to face the opponent. Use this action to help thrust out a reverse punch (**153**);
- Pause, withdraw to a safe distance and resume fighting stance.

This suffers from the same faults as both the previous sequence and nihonme. Re-read the relevant sections.

Figure 153 *Slide your foot back out and turn your hips into a reverse punch to his kidneys.*

Free sparring

In my view, this is the earliest grade at which students can free spar. The following rules are offered for your consideration:

- The best benefits accrue when both partners are not collapsing from fatigue. Tiredness increases the chances of misjudgment, and leads to poor techniques;
- Sparring should not go on and on, and two minutes of actual sparring is optimum. Use a stopwatch to measure elapsed time;
- Do not spar on concrete or tiled surfaces because falling on these can cause serious injury;
- Do not wear spectacles and be extra careful if you use contact lenses as they are apt to pop out in the hurly-burly;
- Remove earrings, necklaces and sharp-edged rings because these can cause injury both to the wearer and to the partner. Tie back long hair with an elastic band — not with a metal clasp! Make sure finger and toe nails are both clean and short;
- Men should wear an approved design of groin protector and women should use a breast shield. Fist mitts must be worn. Shin/instep protectors save bruises and give confidence;
- Spar at half speed but do not mis-use this and seize hold of the partner's slowed-down kick. Try to touch the opponent lightly on target areas and avoid kicks to his groin, knees and insteps;

THE ORANGE BELT SYLLABUS

- Do not make open-hand attacks to the face or strike at the throat;
- Disengage momentarily when the opponent scores on you, recognize his effort with a nod and then resume sparring. By this means, sparring does not turn into a melee of blows and kicks.
- Pull back if things get out of hand and bow to your opponent. Then withdraw from the fighting area.

The Green Belt Syllabus

Introduction

Green belt syllabus introduces no new punches, though it does link a kick and punch sequence which we previously practised as individual techniques. A new kick must be learned and there are four new combinations which exploit it. There are two new head block defences but only one kicking block defence, and you must also learn the katas **pinan sandan** and **pinan yodan**.

Punches

Front kick, lunge punch to head

This is built up of two basic moves and its Japanese name is **kette junzuki-no tsukomi**. Refamiliarize yourself with the basic moves by rereading the earlier sections, then perform the sequence in the following way:

- Begin from left lunge punch stance by performing front kick to mid section. Keep the punching arm still, so the kick thrusts out just below it (**154**);
- Withdraw the kick and set the foot down carefully and without side-step;

Figure 154 *Keep your punching arm extended as you perform a front kick.*

THE GREEN BELT SYLLABUS

- Pull back your left fist and as weight descends on the right heel, thrust out a right lunge punch to the head (**155**);
- On the next command, front kick with your left foot whilst holding your right arm extended. Do not expect to kick too high, because you are leaning forward into the punch.

Avoid the following mistakes:

- Do not kick off centre;
- Do not wave the punching arm about as you kick;
- Keep your shoulders relaxed. This is particularly important because you are still leaning into the previous punch;

Figure 155 *Drop forward and lunge punch to the head. Lean behind the punch but withdraw your chin.*

- Do not let the non-punching arm move away from your side;
- Do not land with side-step or the punch will lose its form;
- Do not desynchronize the kick/punch transition;
- Do not forget to lean into the new punch.

Front kick, reverse punch to groin

This is also made up from two basic techniques linked together.

- Begin from left punch stance by performing front kick to mid section. Keep the punching arm still (**156**);

Figure 156 *Front kick with your punching arm extended.*

Figure 157 *Land with your hips cocked, but leave your arm extended.*

Figure 158 *Thrust your hips forward and perform a reverse punch to the groin.*

- Withdraw the kick and set the foot down scarcely in front of the rear foot but far to the side of it (**157**);
- Pull back your right fist and thrust out a left reverse punch to the groin (**158**);
- On the next command, front kick with your left foot whilst holding your left arm extended. Kick to the side of your arm, so the foot rises above the fist.

Avoid the following mistakes:

- Do not kick below your fist;
- Do not wave your punching arm about during the kick;
- Keep your shoulders relaxed and do not lean back as you kick;

- Do not let the non-punching arm move from your side;
- Do not land without side-step or the following punch will lose its form;
- Do not let your front knee lean inwards;
- Do not let your punching shoulder lean in too far.

The Japanese name for this technique is **kette gyakuzuki-no tsukomi**.

Kicks

Back kick to the knee (**ushirogeri hiza**) must be learned for 5th kyu, and it com-

THE GREEN BELT SYLLABUS

Figure 159 *Maintain your guard and step across with the front foot.*

Figure 160 *Twist your hips fully and look straight ahead. Your back is turned away from the direction in which you will kick.*

Figures 161 *Lift your right foot and thrust it out with the heel leading.*

bines a turning motion of the body with a straight thrusting kick that impacts with the heel. Hip rotation flows seamlessly into the thrusting action.

Begin from left fighting stance and follow this sequence:

- Step across with your front foot (**159**). The distance covered is critical and will only come through practice, but rule of thumb is to cover an equal distance on either side of the stance centre line;

- Twist your hips so you turn your back fully on the opponent and look straight ahead (**160**);

- Lift your right foot and thrust it directly backwards, with the heel leading (**161**);

- Lean forwards but keep your head raised;
- Withdraw the spent kick and put your right foot down so as to set up an effective fighting stance (**162**).

The following are general faults:

- Not stepping far enough across with your front foot so the final stance is too narrow;
- Stepping too far across with your front foot, so the final stance is too wide;
- Letting your elbows flap away from your sides;
- Not turning your hips fully, so the kicking foot and knee do not turn downwards;
- Failing to lean forward, so the kick is too low;
- Letting the head fall forward;
- Not setting the foot down correctly afterwards, so the final stance is badly set up;
- Failing to perform the turn-kick-turn as a smooth sequence.

One-step side kick

One-step side kick (**surikomi sokuto**

Figure 162 *Withdraw your foot and set it down to the side, so you can turn quickly into an effective fighting stance.*

Figure 163 *Step forward and raise your kicking leg, pointing the heel towards the target.*

chudan) uses a one-step accelerator to build up speed and to close distance. Follow this sequence:

- Begin from fighting stance, advancing a step with the left foot so it passes behind the leading foot. This sets up the hips for the following kick;
- Lift the right knee diagonally across the body and point your heel at the target (**163**);
- Thrust your right foot out in one movement, so there is a smooth transition from the step to the kick (**164**);
- Withdraw the foot and set it down carefully.

Figure 164 *Thrust your foot out in a straight line, heel and edge of foot leading.*

Avoid the following errors:

- Stepping in an orthodox scissors step, so the advancing foot passes in front of the shin of the supporting leg. This fails to set up the hips;
- Letting the elbows move away from the sides;
- Making a jerky transition between the step and the kick;
- Not withdrawing the spent foot afterwards, letting it just fall to the floor.

Combination techniques

Green belt requires four combinations, all of which use the newly learned back kick to the knee.

Roundhouse kick to midsection, back kick to knee and back fist

The Japanese name for this technique is **mawashigeri chudan, ushirogeri hiza, uraken jodan**. Follow this sequence from fighting stance:

- Perform a roundhouse kick to midsection, changing your guard as you do so (**165**). Drop the kicking foot well forward and make no attempt to recover your hips;
- Let the body position on landing serve as the stepping across to set up the back kick (**166**). Then turn your hips and thrust out back kick (**167**). Turn your kicking knee down to the floor;
- Recover the spent kick and set it down

Figure 165 *Perform roundhouse kick to mid-section and drop your foot forwards with the hips half turned.*

Figure 166 *If the foot is placed correctly, the body is already half-way positioned for a back kick.*

so as to allow adequate side-step in the new fighting stance (**168**). Turn your hips to face the front but draw back your left shoulder as you perform back fist with your right hand (**169**). This causes the strike to unroll out from the shoulder, giving it extra range and speed;

- Recover the back fist and assume an effective fighting stance.

This is a difficult sequence to perform and requires good balance and co-ordination, the two most difficult parts being when the kicks are set down after they have been used. Roundhouse kick must not be fully withdrawn because if it is set down with the hips already partly turned, it effectively sets up the following back kick. Similarly, the back kick must be withdrawn only slightly before it is set down in such a position as to guarantee an effective new fighting stance.

The following are common mistakes:

- Withdrawing the roundhouse kick fully, so it then has to be re-extended and dropped into the correct position;
- Failing to set the spent kicking foot down in the correct position, so the back kick goes off at an angle;

THE GREEN BELT SYLLABUS

Figure 167 *Thrust out the back kick, keeping your elbows to the sides.*

Figure 168 *Drop the foot so the hips are half-turned to the front. Lift your arm in preparation for back fist.*

Figure 169 *Unroll the back fist out as your rear hip pulls back.*

- Not setting the spent back kick down correctly, so the new fighting stance has too much/insufficient side-step;
- Not turning the shoulders away during the back fist, so the technique lacks both speed and power.

Side thrust kick to mid-section, back kick to knee and reverse punch to mid-section

The Japanese name for this combination

technique is **sokuto chudan, ushirogeri hiza, gyakuzuki chudan**.

Follow this sequence from left fighting stance:

- Perform side thrust kick to mid-section, changing your guard as you do so. Drop the kicking foot well forward and do not recover your hips fully;
- Let the body land so as to set up the back kick, then turn your hips and kick;
- Recover the spent kick and set it down correctly. Use the twisting action as you turn to face forward to power a reverse punch to mid-section;
- Recover the reverse punch and resume an effective fighting stance.

This sequence is easier to perform than the preceding one because it does not mix circular techniques with linear ones.

The following mistakes must be avoided:

- Withdrawing the side kick fully after usage;
- Failing to set the spent kicking foot down correctly, so the back kick is inaccurate;
- Failing to set down the spent back kick correctly, so the new fighting stance is not properly set up;
- Not using the hips to power the reverse punch.

One-step roundhouse kick to mid-section, back kick to knee and back fist

The Japanese name for this technique is **surikomi mawashigeri chudan, ushirogeri hiza, uraken jodan**.

Perform this sequence as for the last but one combination, except that the one-step accelerator makes it unnecessary to change the guard during the first kick.

One-step side thrust kick to mid-section, back kick to knee and reverse punch to mid-section

The Japanese name for this combination technique is **surikomi sokuto chudan, ushirogeri hiza, gyakuzuki chudan**. Perform it as for the basic combination.

Prearranged sparring

Three new prearranged sparring sequences must be learned for the 5th kyu syllabus. Two are in response to a head punch and one responds to a front kick, and they may be performed as either three-step or one-step sequences. Revise the equivalent techniques from the 6th kyu syllabus at this point.

Head block III

This is known as **jodan uke sanbonme** and it continues the Wado Ryu tradition for advanced blocking technique by using a punch which both deflects the opponent's punch and strikes him in the face. Perform it in the following way:

- Step back into right fighting stance as your opponent steps forward into left fighting stance;

- Your opponent steps forward and performs lunge punch to your forehead. If you are performing this as a three-step routine, then step back and head block. Repeat a second time;

- Step back with your right foot so your feet come into line about a shoulder width apart. Use your hips to turn sideways on to your opponent;

- The sideways turning motion powers a straight punch with your left arm, so your forearm glances across the top of the opponent's punch, deflecting it to the side;

- Pull back your left foot slightly and perform a right foot roundhouse kick across the opponent's chest. Pull the spent kick back and set it down before stepping back into fighting stance.

Avoid the following mistakes:

- Beginning from an incorrect distance;

- Not judging the step back correctly, so you withdraw too far from the opponent and your counter-punch falls short;

- Not turning your body fully sideways on to the opponent. Make the smallest target whilst withdrawing your face and head away from danger;

- Not withdrawing your left foot by the correct distance, so your roundhouse kick is delivered from too close a range.

Head block IV

The Japanese name for this technique is **jodan uke yonhonme** and it is the last of the basic head block sequences. In this example, the level of blocking efficiency unaccountably falls back to a more elementary one-pause-two, block then punch sequence. Begin from a right stance, whilst your opponent takes up a left stance, then follow this sequence:

- The opponent performs right lunge punch to your face. Maintain your guard and step straight back, so your feet come into line;

- As your opponent throws his punch, turn sideways on and lean away from him;

- Bat his punch to the side with your bent left elbow, holding the fist close to your armpit;

- Strike the opponent's chest with a left back fist, then twist your hips and slide your left foot diagonally forward and outward, so you drop into a low gyakuzuki stance;

- Bring your right arm up in a ridge hand strike to the opponent's groin, striking with the thumb side of your open hand;

- Pause in this position, then withdraw to a safe fighting stance.

Avoid the following errors:

- Do not step back too far or your elbow block will miss the attacking punch;

- Do not allow the fist of your blocking arm to move out from your armpit and lean back so the blocking forearm is vertical;

- Do not step straight into the opponent, or your advancing foot will foul his leading leg;

- Do not keep your body upright. Lean well forward so your head is below the opponent's outstretched punching arm.

Kicking block V

The Japanese name for this technique is **maegeri uke gohonme**. It uses what is called a stopping block because it actually prevents the opponent's front kick from developing. Begin from left fighting stances and follow this sequence:

- Spring forward as the opponent lifts his right knee;
- Close distance and bar down with your left forearm across the top of his knee. At the same time, reverse punch him to mid-section with your right arm;
- Pause after the punch is made, then withdraw into a fighting stance. Your opponent takes a full step back into a new fighting stance.

The success of this technique depends upon early identification of the front kick and a good drive off the rear leg, so much distance is covered. The front kick is stopped before it can generate force and the opponent caught whilst standing on one leg.

Avoid the following errors:

- Advancing too late, so the kicking foot is moving towards you;
- Failing to bar down on the opponent's knee, so his shin catches you in the groin;
- Failing to punch at the same time that you block. You must punch the opponent before he strikes you, because the element of surprise plays a large part in the success of this technique.

Free sparring

Free sparring is required for the green belt syllabus and you should be able to give a good account of yourself whilst using a whole array of techniques and tactics. Show good control and the correct fighting spirit.

The Purple Belt Syllabus

Introduction

I always think of the 4th kyu purple belt syllabus as marking time between the brown belt grades and the earlier novice grades. Fourth kyu was marked by a green belt in the earliest days of Wado Ryu practice, sharing this colour with 5th and 6th kyu. Now only the 5th kyu belt remains, because many students felt that without a belt colour change, they were not making progress! Fourth kyu is a time for recapping and polishing earlier techniques before jumping off for black belt — now only a year away. There are no new techniques as such to learn, though three earlier kicks are performed to higher targets. There are no new blocks to learn and prearranged sparring consists simply of going back over the head and front kick blocks.

The kata requirement is raised to **pinan yodan** and **pinan godan**, the last in the series.

Kicks

Roundhouse kick to head

Roundhouse kick to head (**mawashigeri jodan**) in the Wado Ryu style invariably means using the instep. Whilst there is no actual bar to using the ball of the foot, classical practice does not teach it. The first requirement for an effective kick is the ability to perform it well to mid-section, and if you cannot yet manage this, kicking to the head will be beyond you! Reread the earlier section on roundhouse kick, then follow this sequence:

- Change your guard and turn your upper body, so you stretch the muscles in your side and load them with energy;
- Raise your kicking knee and bring it around to the front, swivelling freely on the supporting leg. Your shin acts as a bar, preventing the opponent from closing with you;
- Lean back to free your hips, allowing the kicking hip to roll up and over the supporting hip (**170**);
- Snap the lower leg out and allow natural joint elasticity to return it, prior to setting it down.

Almost all of the major faults in roundhouse

kick to the head stem from lack of hip flexibility.

- Do not try to kick with your body upright. This jams the hip movement and can injure the spine;
- Do not lose your guard during the kick;
- Do not try to kick unless your supporting leg has turned at least 100 degrees from straight ahead;
- Do not allow your knee to drop, or turn to face the floor.

Figure 170 *Roundhouse kick to the head requires good hip flexibility. Lean back and maintain an effective guard.*

Figure 171 *Side kick to the head requires yet more flexibility since the action of the kick itself does not give ballistic support.*

Figure 172 *Lean well forward, keeping both arms to your sides and your head up.*

THE PURPLE BELT SYLLABUS

Side kick to head

This technique requires even more hip flexibility than the roundhouse kick because the thrusting action does not help the foot to rise to the correct height. The Japanese name for this technique is **sokuto jodan**. Follow this sequence from left fighting stance:

- Raise your right knee and bring it diagonally forward across your chest;
- Your knee must be raised quite high and your right foot is lifted away from the body and towards the target;
- Pivot on your supporting leg and combine this with a straight line thrust with the kicking foot. Lean away from the kick(**171**);
- Withdraw the spent kick to your chest before setting it down once more.

Assuming that you can perform this technique to mid-section, then hip flexibility alone will limit skill. Generally the kicking knee is not raised high enough and the foot swings in an upwards-travelling arc to the target. Avoid the following errors:

- Failing to draw your kicking knee diagonally up *and across* your body;
- Failing to raise the kicking knee high enough;
- Failing to pivot sufficiently on your supporting leg so penetration is lost;
- Failing to turn your hips sufficiently. You must turn so your back is three-quarters on to the opponent — only then can you produce an efficient thrust.

Back kick to mid-section

Ushirogeri chudan is performed in exactly the same way as the knee kick version, except this time the target is the opponent's stomach. The kick is performed as before except that the degree of forward lean is increased. The following description assumes that you can perform ushirogeri hiza correctly:

- Step across by the correct amount and straight away twist your hips;
- Raise your right foot and thrust it out backwards. Lean well forward but keep your head up, and hold your arms to your sides (**172**);
- Partially withdraw your foot and drop it into the correct position. Hip twist strongly and assume a new fighting stance.

The most common faults of back kick to mid-section arise out of a poor opening side-step. There is also a greater tendency for the arms to move away from the sides as the kick is performed.

Combination techniques

Front kick, roundhouse kick, back kick, reverse punch

The Japanese name for this combination is **maegeri chudan, mawashigeri chudan, ushirogeri chudan, gyakuzuki chudan**. Some schools ask for roundhouse kick to be performed to the head. Follow this sequence from a left fighting stance:

- Snap kick with the right leg and change your guard as you do so (**173**). Withdraw your foot and then set it down in a forward position;

- Pivot on your supporting leg and perform a left foot roundhouse kick to the head (**174**), or to mid-section. Withdraw the foot and set it down so the hips are turned ready for the back kick;

- Go straight into a back kick (**175**), setting your foot down afterwards so you can turn powerfully into the reverse punch (**176**);

- The reverse punch is the most power-

Figure 173 *Change your guard and perform front kick.*

Figure 174 *Twist on your supporting leg and perform roundhouse kick to the head.*

Figure 175 *Thrust out back kick to mid-section.*

THE PURPLE BELT SYLLABUS

Figure 176 *Finish with a reverse punch.*

- Begin from left fighting stance with a right foot roundhouse kick. Retrieve the spent kick and set it down with the foot turned outwards to facilitate the following side kick;
- Swivel on your right foot and thrust out a side kick to mid-section. Drop the spent kick so your hips are partially turned for the following back kick;
- Thrust out the back kick and set it down across and behind the supporting leg;
- Twist your hips around and perform a left reverse punch.

Other combination techniques

There are two other combinations to learn but these differ from the first two only insofar as each begins with a step.

ful of the four techniques and is assisted by the body turning behind it.

Roundhouse kick, side kick, back kick and reverse punch

In some schools the opening roundhouse kick is replaced by a front kick. The name of the combination technique in Japanese is **mawashigeri chudan** (or **jodan**), **sokuto chudan, ushirogeri chudan, gyakuzuki chudan**. Follow this sequence:

Prearranged sparring

Revise the previously learned combinations.

Free sparring

Continue to improve your ability to spar in a controlled and skilful fashion.

The First Brown Belt Grade

Introduction

In some styles of karate, the first brown belt is replaced by a blue belt, while in others the brown belt is modified with a wavy white line. Neither of these alternatives is found in classic Wado Ryu karate and the three brown belt grades are all that now exist of the original three colour system.

The 3rd kyu brown belt introduces one new basic technique, and some non-classical schools also teach a reverse roundhouse kick, an import from Korean fighting arts. The combinations rework the basic techniques which we have learned in the earlier grades, though at some stage the formal sequences which I have described are taught.

Prearranged sparring gives way to what is inappropriately named 'basic sparring' (**kihon kumite**), for basic it certainly is *not*! Kihon kumite is found in other karate styles where it does actually refer to an elementary form of practice, but in the Wado Ryu system it raises the level of practice and presents it as something that looks very much like free sparring. There are many sets of prearranged sparring, but in this book we will consider only the first two.

The kata requirement for 3rd kyu is **ku shanku**, the longest of all the karate katas, and it includes most of the techniques used in the Wado Ryu syllabus. As an aside, Ku Shanku is an excellent whole-body endurance training system.

Punches

You will be asked to perform kette junzuki, kette gyakuzuki, kette junzuki-no tsukomi and kette gyakuzuki-no tsukomi. In addition, you will be required to practice **nagashizuki**, the hip-twist snap punch.

Hip-twist snap punch

This technique is very similar to the snap punch which we performed for orange belt and it is worth taking a few moments to review that technique. Nagashizuki also starts like snap punch, advancing the foot into **shizentai** stance, and lowering the fists on to the front of the thighs. Follow this sequence:

- Thrust with the left leg and lift weight off the right, so it skims forward a good pace (**177**). Turn the foot inwards as it comes to a stop;

THE FIRST BROWN BELT GRADE

Figure 177 Slide the leading leg forward a good pace. Raise your fists in preparation for the punch.

Figure 178 Twist your hips as you perform the punch, dragging the rear foot around in an arc.

- Raise both fists as you slide forward, the right leading the left;
- Thrust the right fist forward, using this action to turn the hips behind the punch. If this is done with sufficient force, then the heel of the left foot will slide around so it comes into line with the heel of the right;
- Lean well into the punch and carry the left fist across the chest (**178**);
- Allow natural elasticity to snap the fist back, pause, and then step around and up with the left foot, so hidari shizentai is resumed.

We encountered a version of this technique in the last but one of the head blocks. It is a classical Wado Ryu move in that it combines body evasion with an economy of block and punch. The leading foot must turn in slightly to set up the line for the finished punch and the more the front foot is turned, the more the stance must change. The body leans well forward in a straight line and much of the body weight lies over the leading foot, which allows the rear foot to swing freely to the correct position.

Avoid the following mistakes:

- Do not step with the leading foot facing straight ahead or the hip twist component will be lost;
- Do not turn the leading foot too much, or you will be obliged to twist around too far in the stance;
- Do not lead with your chin;
- Do not immediately recover the spent punch. Wait for a second or two before stepping around slowly and deliberately to resume the starting stance once more.

Kicks

Wado Ryu includes a peculiar jumping kick within its syllabus at this point. Its name is **nidangeri jodan** or 'two stage kick to the head', and it is sometimes practised as a double kick. Begin from left fighting stance and follow this sequence:

- Bring the right leg forward and up, as though you were going to step on to a chair;
- Step on the make-believe chair and jump up to kick with the left leg. Use a front kick and strike with the ball of the foot;
- Withdraw the kick sharply and land on the balls of your feet.

You must begin the kick even as you are stepping on the imaginary chair. Do not leave it too late or your kick will not strike home whilst you are still in flight. Avoid the following mistakes:

- Do not flap your arms about;
- Do not fail to lift your right foot high because this action helps the following jump;
- Do not wait until you have stepped before beginning the kick, or you will squander both height and flight time;
- Do not land flat-footed and awkward.

Reverse roundhouse kick

Reverse roundhouse kick is a non-classical technique now taught so widely in Wado Ryu karate that it has become incorporated into the syllabus of many schools. The kick is named **mawashi-uchi** though it is also known as **gyaku-mawashigeri**. It first appeared in Wado Ryu during the late 1960s, and its earliest publicized appearance in Europe was made by Teruo Kono, 8th Dan.

The Wado Ryu form of this kick is typically performed with a step-up, or a reverse scissors move which takes the rear foot behind the supporting leg. The latter covers more distance and generates more power. Take up fighting stance and follow this sequence:

- Step up and behind with your left foot whilst maintaining an effective guard (**179**);

THE FIRST BROWN BELT GRADE

- Lean back and arch your body so you pre-stretch the muscles in your spine;
- Lift your right foot clear of the floor and raise the knee up across your chest

Figure 179 *Step up and behind the rear leg. Maintain your guard as you do so.*

Figure 180 *Raise your right knee to your chest and turn your hips away.*

(**180**). Extend your right knee joint so the leg straightens as it curves heel-first towards the target (**181**). Hip action is responsible for taking the foot into the target;

- Slightly flex your right knee as the heel approaches the target (**182**). This produces the characteristic hooking action, speeds the final stages of the kick and begins to pull the body upright (**183**);

- Draw the spent kick back to your chest and regain an upright stance with the right leg now leading as quickly as you can.

Figure 181 *Straighten your leg out as it swings around.*

Figure 182 *Strike with the heel, whilst leaning away from the kicking action.*

Figure 183 *Hook back with the heel and gather the leg close to your body before returning to an upright posture.*

Usual target for the kick is back of the opponent's head, his temple, or sometimes the kidneys. Impact is made with the back of the heel, but owing to the difficulty in controlling impact it is more usual to use the sole of the foot in the dojo.

Avoid the following mistakes:

- Do not try to kick from a low knee position;
- Do not kick with leg action alone. It is necessary for the kicking hip to unroll away from the action and the back to arch to develop maximum range. Then fine distance is adjusted by flexing or straightening your right knee joint;
- Do not drop your head. If you have set up the kick correctly, you will find that you are sighting over your right shoulder.

Combination techniques

There is a tendency in most schools of Wado Ryu to dispense with formal combination techniques from this point onwards, concentrating instead on performing those devised by the coach. However, we will consider two basic and formal combination techniques which rely upon the newly-learned hip twist snap punch.

Hip twist snap punch, reverse punch

The Japanese name for this combination is **nagashizuki jodan, gyakuzuki chudan**. Begin from left fighting stance and follow this sequence:

- Step forward with the right foot, turning it inwards to set up the hip twist snap punch;
- Perform hip twist snap punch, turning your hips behind the action and striking with your right fist;
- Step to the side with your right foot and withdraw your right fist, using this to help thrust out a left reverse punch to mid-section;
- Withdraw the reverse punch and settle into right fighting stance.

This is quite a sophisticated sequence, relying on a double hip twist to power two fast punches. The first advance takes you out of the attacker's line and snaps a fast punch into his face, then the second drops you under his guard for a strong punch to mid-section. Avoid the following mistakes:

- Do not just perform a snap punch. Ensure that you step out of line as you deliver nagashizuki;
- Do not try to perform reverse punch from nagashizuki stance. You must side-step with the front foot to set up your hips correctly.

Front kick, hip twist snap punch, reverse punch, roundhouse kick to the head

This combination has the Japanese name **maegeri chudan, nagashizuki jodan, gyakuzuki chudan, mawashigeri jodan**. Begin from left fighting stance and follow this sequence:

- Perform front kick with your right foot

Figure 184 *Perform front kick but do not change your guard.*

Figure 185 *Land forward and thrust out hip twist snap punch.*

(**184**) and set it down in a forward position, turned inwards to set up the following punch;

- Use the energy of landing to thrust out hip twist snap punch (**185**), then step to the side (**186**) and perform reverse punch to mid-section (**187**);
- The left reverse punch takes weight off the rear foot and makes it possible to lift the leg quickly into a roundhouse kick to the head (**188**);
- Withdraw the kick and set it down.

Some schools add a second reverse punch to mid-section at this point.

Prearranged sparring

As I mentioned in the introduction, we move now into the **kihon kumite** series, with two techniques which are made in response to a head punch.

THE FIRST BROWN BELT GRADE

Figure 186 *Then slide your leading leg to the side and cock the hips.*

Figure 187 *Use hip action to perform reverse punch.*

Figure 188 *The reverse punch lifts weight off the rear foot, so lift and swing it around into a roundhouse kick.*

Kihon kumite I

Face your opponent in formal stance, perform a standing bow and then move into get ready stance, with feet separated by a shoulder width and hands clenched into fists. Your opponent steps forward into right fighting stance and you simultaneously step back into right stance. Both of you must use kiai as you move. Then follow the sequence:

- The opponent moves warily towards you until there is about one fist width between your leading fists, then he settles;
- He then thrusts off his left foot and delivers a long ranging lunge punch to your face. You withdraw your right foot and turn sideways on into a straddle stance;
- Block his punch with your right forearm, bending the elbow so the fist is close to your head. Bring your left fist across your chest where it acts as a guard (**189**);
- Your opponent makes ready to perform a reverse punch with his left fist to your

THE FIRST BROWN BELT GRADE

mid-section; as he begins, step forward with your left foot and maintain your blocking arm (**190**);

- As he punches, swivel around on your left foot, dragging the right around at the same time. Your right arm drops and contacts his punch, guiding it away from your body;

- Use the same hip twist to drive out a short jolting thrust punch into his solar plexus, extending your middle knuckle to make the strike more effective (**191**);

- Pause, then both of you take full steps back into fighting stance. Regard each other for a couple of seconds, then simultaneously draw back into get ready stance once more.

Figure 189 Slide back and turn your body sideways into a straddle stance. Block with your flexed elbow.

Figure 190 Step out to the side as the opponent makes ready to perform reverse punch.

Figure 191 Deflect his punch and simultaneously strike him a short jolting punch to his solar plexus. Use one-knuckle fist.

Figure 192 *Slide back as before and block with your elbow.*

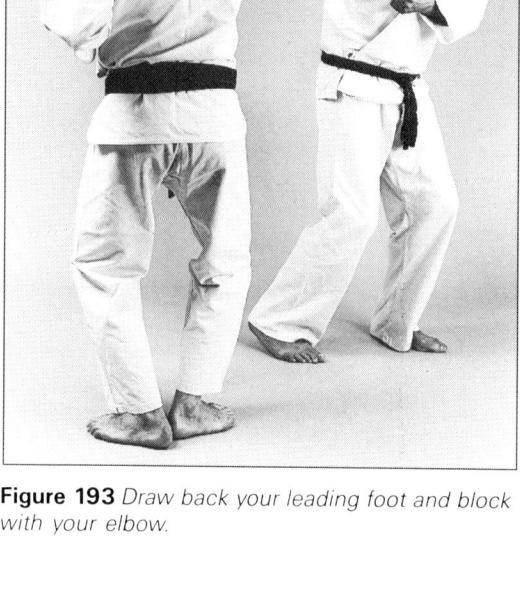

Figure 193 *Draw back your leading foot and block with your elbow.*

This is an extremely difficult routine to master and requires a very fast step to beat the opponent's second punch. The turning action provides power both for a deflection block and for the thrust punch but it requires careful placing to bring your body out of danger. Note how the feet turn unequally, the left rotating more than the right, while both knees bend equally.

Kihon kumite II

In many ways this is a simpler technique to master in that there is a longer gap between the opponent's two attacks, so you have time to prepare. The sequence begins in the same manner, then:

- The opponent slides forward and punches to your face. You slide back and turn your hips as before, blocking with your right forearm (**192**);

- This time the opponent steps up to his leading foot as you draw back your right foot. Note that he leaves his fist extended and you maintain your blocking hand (**193**);

- The opponent performs side kick to mid-section and you pull your right foot in, whilst deflecting the kick with a

Figure 194 *Deflect the opponent's side kick with* **uchi harai uke**.

THE FIRST BROWN BELT GRADE

lower parry. Lean away from the kick and lock your right knee into the left (**194**);

- Allow the opponent to land and slide your right foot back, so it bumps against the back of his right leg. Make a right ridge hand and support it with your left palm (**195**);

- Rotate your hips sharply, so you jar his front leg forward, and at the same time turn your hips behind a ridge hand strike to the base of his shoulderblade (**196**);

- Pause, then take a full step back and conclude as in the previous routine.

194

Figure 195 *Slide your foot back into the opponent's calf. Form ridge hand and support it with the palm of your other hand.*

Competition

Wado Ryu pioneered the concept of karate competition and held the first ever match during the 1930s. Hironori Ohtsuka felt that karate should be adapted in such a way that karateka could safely test their valour and technique in a combat sport environment, but this was so strongly resisted by more traditionalist elements that the disagreement caused Ohtsuka to leave his parent organization and to found Wado Ryu. All the major schools of Japanese karate now hold competitions.

It is therefore appropriate that the stu-

THE FIRST BROWN BELT GRADE

Figure 196 *Turn your hip into a strike to his shoulder blade. This also rotates your leading knee into the back of his, jarring him off balance.*

dent of Wado Ryu becomes acquainted with competition and it is my view that brown belt third kyu is the earliest that this should be attempted. By now, the karateka will have been practising free sparring for at least three months — more like a year in many schools! — and will therefore be able to make an easy transition from the rough and tumble of sparring to more rigidly controlled competition.

Regrettably there is insufficient space in this book to consider the rules of competition in detail but the following will serve as a basic introduction:

● Karate competition can involve both

sparring and kata performance;

- There are both individual and team events;
- Team sparring is single sex and uses five men and two reserves, or three women and one reserve. Team kata is also single sex and fields three men or three women;
- Individual sparring bouts last for two minutes of actual fighting time, though senior male bouts may be extended to three minutes.
- A bell or buzzer tells the competitors when there are 30 seconds left and when time has expired;
- The object is to land a controlled and technically good technique on the opponent's body or head. Excellent techniques score one point and those which are slightly imperfect merit a half point.
- The bout is won when either contestant scores a total of three points. If neither competitor scores the full three points, then the bout will be given to the one with the higher points score, and if this is equal a decision may be made on the relative fighting abilities. Team matches are decided by the team with the higher bouts-win tally. If this is equal the points of each bout are added up. If the tie persists, a deciding bout is fought;
- Draws are permitted in team matches but individual bouts must produce a winner. A tie breaking extension bout is fought and the first to score wins the match;
- Scores are awarded by a referee assisted by a judge and they are both free to move within the competition area;
- The referee can issue warnings, impose penalties and disqualify those competitors who break the rules. Penalties take the form of half or full points added to the opponent's score. Most common rule infringements are failing to control the force of a technique, so the opponent is injured, and stepping outside of the match area;
- Kata matches are held over three rounds. The first round selects the 16 best performers, the second round selects eight and the final round produces the winner;
- Scores are awarded for kata performance by four judges and a chief judge. The highest and lowest scores are deleted and the others are added together. In the event of a tie, the lowest scores are added back in, if the tie persists the highest scores are added in, and if the scores are still level the two competitors must perform a tie-breaker kata;
- Each competitor selects a kata from an official list of 16 which may be performed. A different kata from the list may be performed in the second round, and the third round allows a completely free choice.

Brown Belt Second and First Kyu

No new basic techniques are introduced at this stage and combinations nowadays tend to be decided by the individual coach. Emphasis shifts on to kata and **nai hanchi** is required for 2nd kyu, **chinto** for 1st kyu. Nai hanchi is a curious kata consisting only of sideways movements. Various explanations are given for this, all of them unconvincing, but it is most likely that the kata is all that remains of a more comprehensive training medium for strengthening the legs. This is not surprising when one realizes that early karate styles were cobbled together from a variety of sources, seemingly without regard for the original purpose.

Chinto is also an unusual form, showing quite clear links with northern Chinese kung fu, which when one considers that karate's most used source of technique was southern kung fu, looks curious. However, many and diverse were the contributions made by early martial arts visitors to Okinawa and such a contradiction is at least explainable on that basis. The form uses large movements and is characterized by 'crane on the rock stance' where one foot is lifted clear of the floor and held there for moments of time.

Ku shanku remains the staple underpinning of advanced kata practice and is continued through to the black belt. This long kata is first rate for building stamina as well as for improving skill and the would-be black belt is urged to devote a good amount of time to it. Neither should be pinans be forgotten, because most black belt gradings require a demonstration of all five.

The prearranged sparring sequences must be revised and refined and those kihon kumite sequences appropriate to grade should be learned. Sadly, kihon kumite is dropping out of practice and with it is going one of the most characteristic elements of Wado Ryu karate. Some schools also practise a more extended form of prearranged sparring known as **ohyo kumite** which consists of several different attacking moves performed in a realistic manner, but since it is not universal I have not included examples in this book. Similarly, what is termed **jiu ippon kumite** has not been described, because it exists in as many forms as there are Wado Ryu techniques. Briefly, the attacker is given a single technique to perform on the left or right side and the defender has a free choice of responses.

Glossary

(Words are arranged in the approximate order of their appearance in training)

Rei Bow
Seiza Kneel
Sensei ni rei Bow to the teacher
Otagai ni rei Bow to classmates
Kiritsu Stand up
Nori Stand with heels together, hands flat on thighs
Yoi Stand with feet apart and hands closed into fists
Kihon Basic punches and strikes
Junzuki hidari gamae Take up left lunge punch stance
Junzuki Lunge punch
Mawatte Turn
Jodan uke Head block
Kiai Shout
Sono bade ippon toru Punch without stepping forward
Gyakuzuki Reverse punch
Mawatte gedan barai Turn and lower parry
Yamei Draw back to yoi position
Keri (Geri) Kicks
Hidari hanmei gamae Take up left fighting stance
Maegeri Front kick
Surikomi maegeri One step front kick
Mawashigeri Roundhouse kick
Sokuto fumikomi Stamping kick to the knee
Renraku waza Combination techniques which link basic techniques together into a series
Uke Blocks
Chudan soto uke gyakuzuki Middle section outer block, reverse punch
Chudan uchi uke gyakuzuki Middle section inner block, reverse punch
Junzuki-no tsukomi Forward leaning lunge punch to face
Gyakuzuki-no tsukomi Forward leaning reverse punch to groin
Sokuto chudan Side kick to mid-section
Sanbon kumite Three-step prearranged sparring
Ippon kumite One-step prearranged sparring
Pinan A series of elementary karate kata
Kata A series of combination techniques and individual basic techniques performed in series to a pre-set order
Nukite Spear hand
Shuto Knife hand
Tettsui Hammer fist

Kette junzuki Kick, lunge punch

Kette gyakuzuki Kick, reverse punch

Surikomi mawashigeri One-step roundhouse kick

Surikomi sokuto chudan One-step side kick to mid-section

Tobikomizuki Snap punch

Kette junzuki-no tsukomi Kick, leaning forward lunge punch to face

Kette gyakuzuki-no tsukomi Kick, leaning forward reverse punch to groin

Ushirogeri hiza Back thrust kick to knee

Jiu kumite Free sparring

Nagashizuki Hip twisting snap punch

Nidan geri jodan Double kick to the face

Ushirogeri chudan Back kick to mid-section

Mawashigeri jodan Roundhouse kick to head

Sokuto jodan Side kick to head

Mawashi-uchi Reverse roundhouse kick

Kihon kumite Basic sparring

Shotokan Karate

In this comprehensive training manual, martial arts expert David Mitchell explains clearly and concisely:

- the origins of Shotokan
- how to find and join a Shotokan club
- learning and improving basic kicks, punches and blocks
- analysing technique and identifying faults
- linking moves into combination techniques of increasing complexity
- safe and effective sparring
- competition and tactics

Over 150 photographs amplify the step-by-step instructions and help the reader to achieve effective self-monitoring of technique, even in the absence of a coach. The depth of technical analysis and concise and practical presentation make this the essential Shotokan handbook.

David Mitchell started the first university karate club in Britain in 1965, and has been involved with the practice, control and administration of the sport ever since, right up to Olympic level. He is a leading author on martial arts topics and is endorsed by the British Martial Arts Commission, the 'watchdog' of good practice.